DEXTER'S DIARY

JOANNE JARVIS

AND CO.

CONTENTS

How many angels are there?
One who transforms our lives is plenty

— TRADITIONAL SAYING

*"To all animal lovers
and the animals that we love"*

ACKNOWLEDGMENTS

I am forever thankful to everyone that has supported me. There are plenty of people and animals that helped bring this book to fruition.

First and foremost, with gratitude and love, I have to start by thanking Dexter. He gave me these words and is unfailingly my strength and motivation. You couldn't be more loved. Dexter's Diary is testament and tribute to you and everything that you taught me. I could say 'thank you' a million times and it still wouldn't be enough...

My beloved Mum, who's memory will also always be eternal, thank you for believing in me and for keeping Dexter company until we are all together again.

Richard, my dear husband, whom I so appreciate reading all the drafts (he's no book worm by any means), sourcing photographs and assisting with I.T. I am not at all 'technical' and do not believe that Dexter's manuscript would be together without you. Your patience, love and unflinching loyalty, every single step of the way is treasured.

I am ever so thankful to our little Daisy Cat, Co-writer and the ultimate task master, it hasn't gone unnoticed that Daisy has very much been instrumental in keeping me going and focused on writing, right through to completion. I am much obliged to all teachers and mentors (animal and human) that have guided and assisted me over the years. I'm so grateful for having learned so much from you.

Many Thanks to my family and dearest friends, who all knew that I could do this, and without whose loving support and encouragement, I could not have finished *Dexter's Diary*. In particular, I am beyond grateful to Sarah for invaluable advice and painstaking attention to detail with regard to grammar. Also Debz for her super-speedy typing of a fair few chapters, when my physical health wasn't up to the job. Thank you both for your long-standing friendship and for endless, positive words of encouragement. Along with Kate (my sister), Janice, Cheryl, Sue, Sal, Fiona and Lisa. The Smith, Jarvis and Stoneman families, especially my nieces and nephews, Charlotte, Tom, Millie, Harry, Ellie, Jessica and Isla, all deserve a mention too.

Deepest appreciation to my dad, Michael and all at Authors and Co. I sincerely thank you for your assistance in helping me bring this book to the world. Including of course Tim, most talented designer for all your expertise and patience in honouring our beautiful boy Dexter with such a gorgeous cover.

Finally, the support of those who share my intense love and respect for animals is of great value to me. Animals are my life, my passion and I thank those close to me for understanding and putting up with me <u>always</u> putting animals first.

DON'T GET A DALMATIAN!

We went against all the advice given, with the exception of my nephew Tom who was four at the time, and it turned out to be the best decision we ever made...

Until we visited Dexter's place of birth, I had never seen a tiny Dalmatian puppy up close. I was completely taken by the beauty of his proud mother and her adorable pups trotting across the stable yard to greet us. What a stunning picture that was, and something that I will always remember. Lucy (Missy Kintore) was a calm, attractive and petite liver spotted Dalmatian and she had produced a fine litter of nine pups (five black and white, four liver and white). The pups had good breeding and to look at the Kennel Club names on their Pedigree Certificate there was many a noble title amongst the names of the ancestors. Counts, queens, princesses, chiefs, captains and angels were listed in the heritage. The pups' sire (Minstral's Lad) was not there at the stables at this time, but we discovered that he actually lived only a short distance away from us. We had no intentions of showing a dog or using a dog for breeding so Kennel Club registration was unnecessary in our case. Even so, the Kennel Club promotes an 'Assured Breeder Scheme' which encourages good breeding practice and aims to work with breeders and buyers to force puppy farmers out of business, which is certainly a positive.

We had very carefully considered the reality of having a dog. My husband, Richard and I had extensively researched into possible suitable breeds but kept coming back to Dalmatians. We were both drawn to this well known, loyal, playful and energetic breed. A Dalmatian was a good match for our active lifestyle and love of the great outdoors. I have always felt that it is important to be realistic and to have pets that suit your lifestyle. Any pet is a lifetime commitment and we had waited such a long time until circumstances allowed for a dog to be introduced.

Yet, when we discussed our intentions about possibly having a Dalmatian with friends, family and work colleagues, we were disappointed to hear only negative comments....... *"So and so had a Dalmatian and it destroyed the house"*....... *"They are loopy, headstrong and un-trainable"*. *"They shed a LOT of hair!"* The insults went on and on. The *only person (and a small one at that) who was excited and* supportive was Tom, our nephew. He assertively announced that we should in fact "get the Dog and call him Spot".

I had seen Walt Disney's 101 Dalmatians film as a child too. Even now, I love watching the epic adaptations of Dodie Smith's novel, *The Hundred and One Dalmatians*. All those adorable spotty dogs escaping from the clutches of the dastardly Cruella de Vil, utterly fabulous! Admittedly, Roger and Anita ended up with many more puppies than they bargained for and of course this wasn't real life. But could we handle one? Pongo and Perdita were great dogs, after all.

We had, over the years, looked after numerous pets for friends and family, and had heard about a Dalmatian puppy that needed a new home owing to a child's allergy. Disappointingly, when we enquired about the pup, we were told that he had already gone to another home. We hoped that he had found a suitable forever home, but were so upset to have missed out on the opportunity to adopt him. We had set our hearts on a Dalmatian.

So, here we were, totally transfixed by the 'animated' (full of life, not drawn for a film) spotty puppies. These adorable, appealing characters had captured our full attention. They looked rapturously happy, healthy and alert and were playing together perfectly. They were immaculately clean and so was their environment, albeit outdoors. When I knelt down, a gorgeous little liver spotted, confident, yet gentle pup bounded up. He stopped long enough to sniff and inspect me thoroughly whilst letting me take in his beauty. I stroked his soft, striking coat and silky ears; he was super cute and friendly. He then moved over to Richard, who was now kneeling down beside me. This playful, inquisitive pup then leapt onto Richard's knee, climbed up onto his back, carefully reached for the nearby dangling hay net and swung across - what a comedian. We were then joined by the rest of his fun-loving litter mates and what a ball they were all having. The puppies were noticeably enjoying the ongoing interaction with the people on the yard. Also making their own entertainment in a whirlwind of rough and tumble type play (nothing too boisterous) diving on leaves, straw and thoroughly examining the smells throughout the stables.

The party host with a winning personality proceeded to make himself the centre of attention once more. Looking extremely pleased with himself, he pranced around and at our feet he presented us with a champagne cork that he had found! Well, that was it - we got the message loud and clear now. We should celebrate. This pup was bright as a button and we were the chosen few. How would we remember which pup had chosen us? They would develop more markings. Well, that was easy. Dexter was already beautifully marked, even at the tender young age of almost seven weeks. Although he would get more spots, he had a prominent lucky number 7, a pattern in his markings, on his right ear. This was very distinguishable, unique and utterly charming. Gosh he was adorable. He had the most extraordinarily expressive face and such kind, gentle eyes. How I wished I could have taken him home with us right there and then as he gazed lovingly at me.

However, it would simply not be fair to take him now. Dexter still had a lot to learn in the coming weeks from his mother and siblings. Puppies that are separated from their litter mates and their mother too early will often fail to develop important social skills. Interaction in this family unit is incredibly important. It is very sad when puppies are sold and taken away too early, especially as they can sometimes then have issues in later life. Puppies gain massive behavioural benefits even just from playing with their litter mates at this very young age. They learn how far to go in play biting and wrestling through games and begin to understand acceptable limits and manners from their mother and hierarchy of course too.

Richard and I still had some work to do ensuring our home and garden was "puppy proof" and ready for Dexter's arrival. We had longed for a dog for many years but had waited until now. We felt that it would not have been fair to leave a dog alone at home for extended periods of time when we were both previously working such long hours. We fully understood that we should always think of animals' needs before our own, because they rely on us. Our decision to have a dog was not taken lightly. Although I was working full-time, my parents were now retired and lived less than a mile away and had offered to help out regularly. Richard was predominantly self-employed, working flexible hours and at home an awful lot more now too. We wanted our boy to have a lovely life. We wanted everything to be just right for Dexter - he had already won us over.

Richard and I specifically wanted a younger dog so that we could be involved in socialisation and training. A younger Dalmatian would be adaptable and when fully grown, would also enjoy being with an active, outdoor family. Dexter was going to be our first puppy, but we did have some prior knowledge and experience as we had been lucky enough to have pets growing up in our respective homes. Initially, we had met and got together because of our dogs. We were teenagers at the time, on holiday with our families. Richard's dog Sumo was a charismatic character and romanced our Lucy. They were a unique couple for sure. Sumo was a Staffordshire Bull Terrier and Lucy a Golden Retriever. Both were great dogs and had sadly passed away some years ago.

It is disappointing and very sad that some people go out on a whim and purchase a cute puppy without doing any research. I have always said that buying a dog is the easy bit, if you have the money, of course. Perhaps in blissful ignorance, some people appear to lack knowledge of what the responsibility of being a dog owner actually entails. Let alone be aware of the characteristics and requirements of a particular chosen breed or cross-breed. It is the poor puppy that is ultimately disposed of or dispensed with when it grows up and gets "too big", "too energetic" or "unruly". Of course, it goes without saying that there are a lot of genuine reasons for a dog legitimately having to be re-homed. When family and circumstances in a dog's life change and they are separated it must be heart-breaking for both parties.

Over the years, I've encountered people who have declared, "we just didn't have the time/it didn't fit in with the family/it tore the house up". Possibly this happened because circumstances changed and the dog was bored or it wasn't walked enough, mentally stimulated, received no training, socialisation and guidance or received mixed messages? It is upsetting that pets sometimes get passed from pillar to post thinking that they have done wrong. If only people took the time to understand an animal's needs in the first instance there would be fewer unwanted pets in animal shelters and rescue centres.

The next two weeks I was away from home with work, but after that I had booked annual leave so that I could stay at home to help Dexter settle in. For the fortnight I was away on the training courses and seminars, my poor work colleagues must have been driven mad. I am not joking; I have never been so excited in all my life. I would talk about our adorable pup to anyone who would listen. Showing pictures like many a proud parent and, with a new found knowledge of breed information I was armed and dangerous to anyone who dared slur the good name and character of the dashing Dalmatian breed.

Those two weeks passed so slowly. The weekend I returned home, in between the two, we just couldn't resist taking a trip to see how our little boy was coming along. Dexter was physically visibly pleased to greet us, with a look of recognition too. Seeing Dexter and feeling that pang of emotion totally convinced me that we belonged together. He really was our little lad, and boy he had my heart. Wow, I felt like the luckiest person on the planet! Dexter had surprisingly grown quite a bit since our last visit and become even more gorgeous and curious too. Some of the pups had already left their mother and litter mates to go to their new homes. Dexter didn't appear to mind, especially as he was getting more attention and guidance from his mother as a result. Food too, by the look of it!

A supreme, dignified Golden Retriever patrolled the stable yard. He kept the playful young dogs in order, whilst assessing/checking out all visitors. This handsome male was appropriately named Shadow. He then joined my parents, Richard, my sister and I, whilst we observed the remaining inquisitive, bounding Dalmatian pups as they ran excitedly around the yard. Under the watchful eye of their attentive mother, before long they were back inside their stable. Shadow leaned his head against my leg, and as I stroked his long and wonderfully soft coat I was reminded of Lucy, our lovely Golden Retriever.

Soon it was time to head home. We were reluctant to leave and it was a wrench to say goodbye, particularly as Dexter appeared sorry to see us go. When he peeped over the low gate that prevented the puppies escaping from the stable, I remember telling Dexter that I would be back next week without fail to collect him...That day couldn't come soon enough.

"Sunday 5th December, Collecting Dexter today !!!"

SETTLING IN

The day that we had been waiting for had finally arrived. Both our home and garden were puppy proof. I had read numerous books and listened to all relevant advice given and I was on my way with Mum to collect Dexter. Unfortunately, Richard was on a course which had been pre-booked months ago, with the Fire and Rescue Service and was unable to come with me due to these work commitments. As Mum and I set off in the car I could not quite believe that today was the day Dexter was to come home with us. I remember little of the hour and a half journey, although I do recall passing through the market town of Nantwich and seeing an enormous Dalmatian, elegantly trotting alongside its guardian. Dexter would not grow up to be that big though surely? We had remarked how petite his mother was.

When Mum and I arrived at the stable yard, we were

once again greeted by proud mum Lucy; along with her two other remaining pups. One poor little pup was now re-available as the prospective owner must have had a change of heart and had not turned up to collect on the agreed day or even bothered to telephone. How must that little one have felt? After collecting Dexter's papers, food and instructions, it was time to take our boy home. I picked him up, held him in my arms and promised his mother that I would look after him.

Walking over to the car, I was astonished to find that Dexter did not object to leaving his mother and siblings. My mum was already sitting in the back seat of the car, waiting for us. We had Dexter's temporary bed ready there for him (a cardboard box lined with comfortable blankets). We also had a towel positioned by the side of Mum, in preparation for the long journey home. I placed little Dexter in his cosy makeshift bed, but two seconds later he was proudly sitting on Mum's knee. He settled instantly there and slept soundly for the entire journey home. We were prepared for every eventuality, such as travel sickness and toileting needs, but we need not have worried. Throughout the drive home, my concentration left a lot to be desired but Dexter didn't seem bothered. He was a gem, we really were astounded.

When we arrived home I carried him into the garden where he had a sniff around the lawn and by the look of it a much needed wee. I praised Dexter for being so good, his body wriggled and his tail wagged and wagged. He looked somewhat bemused entering the house. He had probably never even been inside a house before. After all, he was raised in a stable. Any potential concerns were hastily dismissed as soon as I started to prepare Dexter's meal. Mum had warned me that he would probably be upset after leaving his family. She commented that it was more than likely that he would not want to eat this meal. Well, how wrong could she have been? This little boy was ravenous and his bowl was empty in seconds. I could not actually believe my eyes either, but was so relieved. Our little pup was obviously happy and settled enough to eat.

Dexter slept on the tiled kitchen floor that afternoon. He had been used to wood shavings in the stable that he'd shared with his mum and siblings. In the evening, when I was preparing our Sunday dinner, Dexter tentatively watched me from his new bed. I do not think that he knew quite what to make of the home environment yet. Or the appetising cooking smells from the food that I was preparing for dinner that evening. However, it certainly did not take this little guy long to work out that this was good. This was just the start of what was going to be a very important time of socialisation and familiarisation for Dexter. What he would experience and learn right now, and in the coming weeks and months would shape his behaviour.

When Richard came home, I did not get so much as a second glance. Dexter was so adorable that no one could possibly resist him. Although, we were sensible, right from the start to ensure that we didn't give mixed messages or signals to Dexter. We folded our arms, turned away and ignored him if he jumped up, for example. He very soon learned that he only got attention and affection (even with the waggiest tail) when he had all four paws on the floor. Some people say 'it's okay' if a cute puppy jumps up. It's not and certainly won't be okay when a dog has grown, particularly a big one. We praised the good behaviour and ignored the bad and encouraged all visitors that were carefully introduced (and there were lots) to do the same.

Remarkably, that first night we did not hear a peep out of little Dexter. He slept soundly in his new home and comfortable bed. Perhaps he was enjoying a life of luxury, sleeping indoors, warm and safe. We were very much comforted to know that he was relaxed and contented. The couple of weeks annual leave that I had taken allowed me to spend time with our boy and settle him into a routine, start housetraining and make sure he was comfortable in his new surroundings. I loved spending time with Dexter. He was such fun and a joy to be around.

It was early December and the weather was fair which was a godsend for housetraining. Unbelievably our clever Dexter only had one little accident, a puddle in the kitchen. Housetraining was a breeze. That first night, I had put down some puppy training pads but

Dexter thought they could be more appropriately used for enjoyment and amusement instead. Tossing them into the air, shredding and dragging them around seemed a real hoot to Dexter, but I was worried that he might possibly digest some of the wadding or plastic, so promptly removed them from the floor.

Instead I invested time, wisely as it turned out, taking him into the back garden frequently, especially after meal times to relieve himself. A tasty treat, lots of praise and affection every time he did what was expected of him certainly paid off. He soon learned to "wee on command" which was especially useful when Richard or myself had to go out unexpectedly or we could see a rain cloud coming. Dexter really did not like the rain. Our little boy was the cleanest puppy I have ever known; perhaps this was because Dexter had lived with his mother and siblings in a stable? After all, he was used to going outside to relieve himself, or maybe it was the training? Dexter really did thrive on training, love, attention, stimulation and reward – especially food reward!

During that first week that we had Dexter, we were extremely calm and patient. We gave him time to get used to his new home and surroundings and unfamiliar things. I decided to take him over to my parents' house that was only a short drive of just a mile across the village. I wanted to get Dexter used to the car and visiting their home since he would spend time there, with my mum and dad whilst Richard and I were at work. Dexter hadn't had his second puppy vaccination yet so he didn't have full protection to go outside of the home and garden environment. Mum and Dad didn't have any pets or unvaccinated pets visiting their home, so Dexter was safe to explore there too.

I do remember thinking, as I placed Dexter in the back of the car, that being so good with me and Mum on his first car journey, that I should not expect any problems. However, I was on my own in the car this time. I started the car, set off and pulled off the drive and onto the main road. In my rear view mirror, I could see a cute little chocolate brown nose and spotty head popping over the back seat. This cute little spotty head was soon followed by a scrambling cute little spotty body and legs. Before I knew it and could find a safe place to stop, Dexter had navigated his way over the seat, through the gap between the driver and passenger seats and was very proudly sitting on my knee. He looked very pleased with himself indeed. I had to laugh at Dexter, he was such a character, totally adorable and just wanted to be close. Seriously though, as cute as he was, I realised that this could not become a regular habit.

To Dexter's disgust and disappointment, we fitted a rear dog guard to our car the very next day. This was for his safety, ours and that of other road users. Nowadays, you can be fined for breaking the law, if dogs are not suitably restrained in a vehicle. Unrestrained, unruly dogs can cause an accident by distracting a person driving a vehicle. Properly fitted seatbelts, harnesses and dog guards ensure that dogs are not moving around and may well save a dog from injury in the event of a crash.

Dexter progressed brilliantly with his socialisation and familiarisation training, but Dalmatians do sometimes have a reputation for being somewhat difficult to train. Possibly this may be due to high energy levels, low concentration and a large percentage, approximately 30 per cent I believe, being born deaf or having bilateral hearing (which is hearing from one ear) or with some other sort of hearing impairment. Dalmatians have this genetic predisposition. Many aspects of personality and needs are influenced by breed. Although, you may be aware that it is not just Dalmatians who can be affected in this way; white dogs in general can also be too. Through research, it is known that albino and white furred, pale skinned animals of any species tend to be affected by problems with the skin pigmentation in the inner ear because of the lack of mature melanocytes which are vital for normal functioning of the inner ear.

The BAER test can be used to evaluate hearing and is a reliable method for determining whether a dog is deaf, and for measuring the extent of hearing loss. Dalmatians that are deaf or have hearing impairments can of course be trained using hand signals and other techniques. Owners therefore need to be prepared for training that may take longer than other breeds of dog, or dogs that have precise hearing.

Dexter, fortunately had acute hearing. He was also very astute. The fact that he could hear the treat tin being lifted off the shelf, in preparation for training, was an obvious advantage. Dexter was so accommodating and eager to learn. Absolutely nothing fazed him at all. He was confident, friendly, playful and gentle as any dog could be. How dare anyone say that Dalmatians or dogs in general for that matter, are stubborn and un-trainable – that's ludicrous!

It was very rewarding and a sheer delight to run through the basics of training together. Dalmatians can be an intelligent and a highly trainable breed. Dexter was outstanding and sitting proudly for treats on his second day with us. Very soon afterwards he was fully competent in commands such as "stay", "down", "come" and "left" or "right" paw. Dexter understood almost instantly which were left and right paws and boy was that cute to see. He was tiny but at the same time had the most endearing temperament. Dexter was wise and switched on. Even at two months of age, he was a star.

On Dexter's first walk out of the confines and safety of our back garden, Richard and I let him off his lead. Dexter bounded through the soft snow which was blissful to see. With a quick "toot" on the whistle and a hint of a well deserved treat; Dexter was straight back at our feet. Bless him, so biddable, looking lovingly up at us with sparkling, bright and adoring eyes.

Tuesday 4th January

"Dexter was a super-star at the puppy party at the vets tonight. Other puppies disgraced their owners with their uncontrollable and mischievous behaviour. Dexter had perfect manners and really impressed the behaviourist. I am so proud!"

3

PUPPYHOOD

From a tiny pup, we kept a diary on Dexter for our own reference and interest. This initially recorded his progress, significant events, puppy training and medical information which also served as a reminder for necessary and routine tasks such as worming and inoculations. In later years, it greatly assisted with monitoring of trends and patterns concerning his health and management.

We enrolled Dexter in a puppy training class when he was young. One session per week for six weeks. The lady running the sessions was impressed to see that Dexter was already competent in all his basic commands, especially as Dalmatians, as she put it, "could be tricky". She was shocked when we told her that he had been allowed off leash on his first walk. Despite him having an excellent recall, apparently this was not the preferred method when training such a young dog. Hmm, well what can I say; we were not about to change our regime. We trusted and respected Dexter and he trusted and respected us.

The trainer and some of the dog owners were extremely bemused at that first training session when Richard and I proudly produced Dexter's toy spider "Suzy" out of our bag. It was quite funny really, especially when all the other owners produced sturdy Kongs, rope and rubber tug toys. "Now surely that is not very appropriate for a young puppy with sharp teeth" we were told. Dexter certainly did not shred any toys, or possessions and we still have Suzy to this very day. He never destroyed a single thing nor was he crated to prevent such occurrences, as I believe many owners are encouraged to do.

Dexter did everything we asked of him, at all of the sessions, always to all commands. Including trotting beautifully and elegantly to heel. He was patient, obedient and eager to please. It did help to have a pocket full of treats ... Dexter was always very perceptive, shall we say. Nevertheless, I felt like a super-proud parent who'd just watched her child complete their first day at school when he passed the puppy course with flying colours.

Our socialisation, training and positive association continued to progress very well out of training class too. We were committed and fully understood from the start, that it was very important to make time to do this, and we started early, as soon as Dexter came to live with us. We were told that from birth to the first fourteen-sixteen weeks is a critical learning and development period. The right socialisation is key to ensuring that a puppy has the best possible chance to grow up to become a happy, well-adjusted dog that feels safe in various environments, with not only other animals but people too. Dexter had a happy demeanour and enjoyed lots of pleasant social interactions. He took every scenario in his stride. Dexter was outgoing, bold and confident but not cocky. He enjoyed new experiences and being part of family activities during this important period.

It was not all plain sailing in these early days though. You might recall Dexter's car journey and short trip over to my parents' house the first week we had him. My parents' car did not have a dog guard either. Surely a little tiny pup could not clamber over the extra large rear seat of a 4 x 4 could he? Well, he tried and succeeded. Gosh, Dexter caused such a commotion one day when Dad took him out in the car. The poor man could not believe his eyes, especially when tissues and papers started flying around the car in front of him. Dexter had, accidently of course, stepped on the window switches which were situated on the large panel between the driver's and passenger's seats which he had activated when he clambered through to be close to Dad. What fun Dexter had jumping around trying to retrieve the tissues and paper. All four of the windows kept going up and down on that blustery day. Dad was powerless to do anything about this until Dexter settled beside him on the centre console, while Dad tried to keep his car on the road. We still have a good chuckle about this incident now (even though dad has a few more grey hairs to remind him).

There were no more occurrences of that nature, fellow road users will be pleased to hear. Mum always sat in the back seat from then on and Dexter was happy to look up at her from the boot whilst she stroked his adorable spotty head and those gorgeous silky ears. He no doubt enjoyed a treat or two for good behaviour and having all four paws on the floor. Mum, Dad and Dexter all enjoyed trips to, from and around the local nature reserve and country park whist Richard and I were out at work.

Arguably one of the most recognisable dog breeds, Dalmatians are generally affectionate dogs that love to be in a social environment. Dexter was a particularly striking puppy and became even more handsome as he was growing (at a tremendous rate). I am sure that he loved all of the attention that he attracted. I was delighted to have him with me and by my side, wherever we went. Dexter was a perfect, well-mannered companion whose charm captivated everyone in some way, shape or form. Always friendly to anyone who would take a moment to talk and interact (animal or human). "Isn't he lovely", was a phrase our loyal little soul became very familiar with indeed. Petting a dog prompts a release of the "feel good" hormones in humans and is a theory that has been gaining notable scientific support for some time. Doing his bit to raise oxytocin levels, Dexter certainly made a lot of people smile.

Of course being personable was an obvious advantage to Dexter too. When we were out and about, people loved to fuss over him and he certainly gobbled all the treats that people gave him with relish (when he was sitting patiently of course). We were so proud of Dexter. Richard, Mum, Dad and I had all been careful and consistent with his training which had definitely paid off. My parents had initially looked bemused when I first handed them a whistle and a copy of Dexter's regime and list of commands. These were to be used when Richard and I were working and little Dexter was entrusted in their care. Nevertheless, we all worked together to ensure that he stayed within the boundaries and limitations set and did not become an unruly Dalmatian.

Dexter was not over stimulated, rather he enjoyed a phased programme of socialisation and habituation. Dexter was exposed to just about any possible scenario but not bombarded. We enjoyed exploring different environments, introducing him to unfamiliar species, new things and creating these positive experiences. This was especially important as Dexter was born and isolated in a stable environment before he came to us.

He had met horses and other dogs but only had limited contact with humans there and not been in a home environment or seen other animals either. Initially, noises like the hoover for example, must have been very strange indeed for Dexter but he was remarkably tolerant. Socialisation and habituation is so important for young dogs. If they don't have this, and just have time in the garden they can sometimes become fearful of unfamiliar situations and stimulus later on in life and it is often then too late to try and train them so that they are not fearful. Sound based treatment programmes are available to help puppies adapt to their life as a pet. These CD's can help to familiarise pets with a collection of sounds, such as traffic, household noises, children and fireworks. When safely and gradually exposed to different experiences, whilst doing something that they enjoy at the same time, hopefully helps dogs to be relaxed and tolerant. Dexter was pretty easy-going and nothing really appeared to bother him. In fact, he loved the sound of a motorbike approaching, most likely because Richard had one.

Social relationships are very important between humans and animals and we stayed focused to ensure that are any misbehaving was handled appropriately and immediately. Most of an animal's bad behaviour is often a result of owners incorrectly perceiving what the pet needs or wants and it is actually very easy to reward bad behaviour without realising. We all really need to see the world from the animal's perspective to ensure that they are properly guided, handled and given proper care.

We were also mindful to ensure that we followed guidelines to ensure Dexter's safety and well-being. Puppies need much less exercise than fully grown dogs even though they are playful and eager to run. A growing puppy can damage its developing joints if it is over-exercised or inappropriately exercised. We were so careful, even to the point that we had a stair gate fitted so that he was not permitted to run up and down the stairs whilst his joints were forming, and he was growing at a radical rate. He never jumped up or "counter surfed" etc. Dexter had regular, sensible exercise and did not have too much vigorous off-lead exercise to protect his developing joints, bones, ligaments and tendons.

Dexter was a playful and happy character and found a funny little way to get our attention when he was a pup. He was fun–loving and had boundless energy and enthusiasm, as do many youngsters. On the odd occasion, Dexter would "help" to tidy things away … hiding shoes and tea towels in a particular tree in the back garden. If caught in the act he would stop in his tracks, look up at you with those beautiful eyes, seemingly appearing to wonder how on earth that could have got there? Then he would proceed to prance around like a performing pony. Just look what I have found. He was a good boy though and, if caught in the act, he would drop the articles he had found/collected immediately. He never chewed anything he wasn't supposed to. "Leave it" and "drop" are crucial commands for puppies. "Leave it" teaches an invaluable lesson in impulse control. "Drop" requests the item is subsequently released.

Although Dexter was given rawhide strips and bones when teething, he preferred to hide them out in the garden, weather permitting of course, unless he was really hungry. This funny, characteristic habit was most probably an instinctive behaviour. I once heard it said that dogs ancestors would naturally dig to cover and protect any excess food as leaving it out in the open would invite rivals to eat it. Richard and I would often peep through the window and watch Dexter tentatively use his paw and neatly move a small area of gravel from the path to one side whilst a chew was put in place. He would then carefully nudge all the stones back into place with his nose, thus concealing his stash – or so he thought. There was always a bit of a giveaway, the mound of gravel left in the middle. Instinctive behaviour to hide the chew or not, Dexter preferred not to get his feet wet or dirty by digging in damp grass or soil, he was such a clean boy. He always went round and avoided puddles too. I have never known a dog quite like him.

Although not usually "a digger" the one thing Dexter did experiment with was a little garden design. One day as a pup, he uprooted a newly planted shrub, carefully mind you; he did not damage the base or roots. Much to the displeasure of Richard who was busy gardening at the time, Dexter happily trotted off, dragging the plant to the other side of the garden, satisfied when clearly it was placed in a more suitable location. Oops! The variety of scents emanating from the freshly disturbed earth must have attracted Dexter's attention; I nearly choked on my lunch as I caught a glimpse of a moving bush as he sneaked past the open French doors that overlooked the garden.

And we absolutely must not forget the incident with the sock. Dexter once 'came across' a tiny child's sock that was stuck in the bottom of a friend's daughter's Wellington boot, unbeknown to her parents. The little girl was only young at the time and had said that she had seen Dexter playing with her sock after he had tossed her welly into the air, after we returned from a walk one afternoon. No-one could understand what she meant and it was confusing since she was actually wearing a pair of socks. We soon found out – well nine days later to be precise, when the mystery of the sock was revealed, reappearing as if by magic from some-where unmentionable! All I can say is that I had a real shock picking up his poop and thank goodness the small sock passed through. That and the pound coin and two pence piece I discovered on another occasion. And before you ask, as everyone always does – no I did not clean it off and spend the money!

The Dalmatian was once a popular circus dog. With

their dramatic, eye catching markings and intelligence one can understand why. One sunny Sunday morning, after only two tries at rearing up, Dexter was off, proudly walking around the big conifer tree on his hind legs! He had figured out himself that from an elevated stance he could peep in at the nesting pigeons. Richard and I were dumfounded at what we saw. Dexter was inquisitive and such a comedian at times. We were careful not to let his little mischievous antics go too far in case he got mixed messages or injured himself. He was never boisterous and knew the boundaries which he was encouraged to conform to. We had mutual respect. Dexter was wise and dignified even as a youngster. Calm and always respectful of humans, birds and other creatures.

We discovered during puppyhood that Dexter had a talent for singing. This was quite a shock at first. He would stand proudly as if performing to an invisible audience; singing (or some might say howling) in tune to classical tracks especially. Dexter had a repertoire of favourite songs. His party piece being the classical "The Flower Duet" for which he performed exceptionally and routinely every time we played that particular number or it was aired on the television or radio. This is a popular piece since it was adapted for the theme "Aria on air" for the British Airways advertisement and also appeared on many classical compilations at that time. My little nieces and nephews especially loved to hear Dexter sing. He was always up for an encore, which pleased them enormously. He scared Mum once who actually thought he was in pain, but Dexter was only 'singing'.

Dexter proved to be a brilliant retriever and developed a talent for football too. Utilising his athletic charisma, he liked to skilfully dribble and kick the ball back to us which was intriguing to see and enjoy with him. He would very often pick up a ball, a small football being his firm favourite and gently squeeze it in his mouth corresponding to the number we said. He was such a super, intelligent and delightful little lad.

Dexter demonstrated that pets are very observant and have extra-ordinary senses. Even as an affectionate and sometimes hilarious youngster, he amazed us with his uncanny psychic ability. Sensing that we were coming home, or relatives, visitors and even the postman or window cleaners were soon to arrive. Dexter was always spot on and most discerning of character as well. He showed us that animals can read personality and are empathetic, even at a young age. When those around us fail to notice, pets pay very close attention and can sense what we are feeling and how we are feeling. They are very perceptive and we could all do well to take note.

"Saturday 8th January

"Me and Mum took Dex to the pet shop today. He wasn't frightened of the automatic doors or slippy floor and made loads of friends in store. We were there for ages. Chuffed to bits that he was so well behaved - until he practically inhaled the bowl of dog food that was part of the display. He is so greedy! Mum was mortified. The kibble was filthy and covered in dust!"

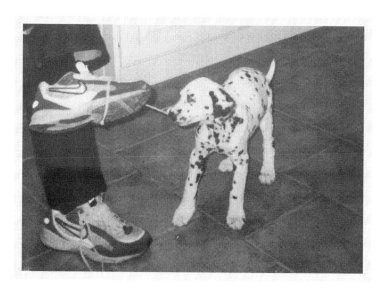

4

SPOT THE DOG

Richard and I had always enjoyed getting out and about on our bicycles in the countryside. We lived next to a bridle path that was accessible from our home. Once Dexter's bones had fully developed, this stretch of perfectly flat terrain was ideal for Dexter to also stretch out and safely exercise, at a smooth gentle pace. He so enjoyed trotting elegantly alongside our bicycles. One can easily see why the energetic Dalmatian breed was chosen during the Regency period to gracefully trot alongside the horse-drawn carriages. The legendary 'Spotted Coach Dog' would also guard the stables at night. With their stunning spotted coats and athletic build they held a very high status.

As well as being a popular coaching dog, the use of Dalmatians carried over to the horse-drawn fire pumps that fire fighters rode to the scene of fire. The Dalmatian's affinity to horses made this breed a natural guardian, running ahead of the engines to quickly clear a path and guide the horses on the move. These dogs served as brave, loyal watchdogs and protectors for the crew and fire stations.

Dexter only ever barked if there was a legitimate need to do so. He was ridiculously welcoming and friendly to anyone who came to the house invited – perhaps because he was positively encouraged to wait in his bed until we gave him the signal to greet (he was initially given a treat in the training phase). One night we suddenly woke hearing Dexter bark. This was a very different, intense, persistent bark which we had not heard before. When I went downstairs to investigate, followed closely behind by Richard, we discovered an intruder in the garden. Dexter had alerted us, he woke us for the first time ever and with very good reason. Richard opened the kitchen doors and the man ran off over the back fields seeing Dexter dashing outside. The intruder was clearly not going to hang around hearing that commotion. Our neighbours were most appreciative of Dexter's efforts.

Dalmatians are an active 'high energy' breed and a perfect choice for people who live in the countryside. We fully understood that the breed require lots of regular, sensible daily exercise and mental stimulation. Dexter and I thoroughly enjoyed our suitable walks. We were becoming inseparable, going everywhere together, whenever I wasn't working and it was possible. In the village where we live, Dexter was extremely popular and a familiar sight, often seen out and about and around the area. Dexter loved exploring environments and socialising. He made lots of friends. Dexter did not mind what species or colour they were, if they had two or four legs, fins, fur or feathers. He was a beacon of light, bringing joy to absolutely everyone and anyone.

Quite by chance, I discovered that Dexter had quite a number of relatives living in the local area. One day he asked to go into the local veterinary centre (that's not a typo) he actually asked by pulling on the leash to drag me in, something he never usually did. At that moment, there was another sharp, heavy rain shower looming so I did not object to this, and in any case we needed to place an order for another bag of food which we always purchased from the veterinary practice at that time.

As soon as we went through the door I could not quite believe my eyes ... sitting in the middle of the reception area floor was a Dalmatian, albeit much smaller than my youngster, black spotted with blue eyes. Dexter looked like he had seen a long lost brother and by Jove the two of them appeared overjoyed to be reunited. It did not cross my mind for one moment that they were actually brothers. We lived in Cheshire and Dexter was from the Welsh borders. Interestingly, when we started to chat, we realised that they were actually littermates. Dexter knew this of course and some years later I heard this fact confirmed on a television documentary that dogs do of course recognise their siblings and why wouldn't they? How clever and intuitive animals are, some people just don't realise.

I looked at Dexter's beautiful face, full of grace and knowing and deserving of awe. He knew, for one thing, what he was. His brother, Charlie. He was there, right there. I only wished that Dexter's brother had a family that understood and appreciated his needs at that crucial learning period too. Sadly, he was confused, undisciplined and the family were struggling to cope. I encouraged the family to come along to training classes with us, and they did just the once. It is sad that some people have not got time available to put in the effort needed, to give young exuberant animals the guidance, training, exercise, boundaries and socialisation that are so important at this stage in their lives. Fortunately for Charlie incidentally, he was given up and re-homed to a lady who understood the Dalmatian breed, temperament and exercise requirements.

Dexter had two black spotted half sisters living nearby. One called Abby and another one called Angel, both living at opposite ends of the village and their respective owners were totally unaware that they were related until we discussed their parentage. Trouble, Dexter's dad had fathered both these girls and it was only by chance that we discovered the connection.

Abby's guardian and I sometimes walked our two

dogs together whilst they were youngsters and boy did they have fun on our outings. It was delightful to see them run and play. They got on like a house on fire. From a distance Abby and her guardian were sometimes mistaken for Dexter and me and vice versa. I didn't mind, she was almost ten years younger than me. It got a bit confusing when an elderly chap who was the husband of a friend of my Mother's, kept insisting that he had told me such and such. He hadn't! Abby's guardian confessed at a later date that she got so fed up of the old man (who is a lovely by the way) thinking that she was me and Abby was Dexter, that she just used to nod politely so that she might promptly go about her business when he had finished talking.

Dexter, Richard and I enjoyed lots of walks, the three of us together, especially on weekends. Dexter particularly liked to sniff out truffles around the higher points in the tranquil woodland that were a little further afield. Our little "snout nav" always promptly located and devoured them, giving no hint of sharing. Richard desperately wanted to try one but there was no chance of that. Gone in a flash. People we met walking in these woods, sometimes mentioned that they thought they had seen Dexter out walking with another couple. This must have been yet another case of mistaken identity for Dexter our Dalmatian. Once, Dexter and I were out on what we hoped to be a relaxing walk together in the same location, but unsuspectingly ended up braced

in the woods, behind a fallen tree. Dexter stood stead-
fast, protecting us from a hunt that unexpectedly and
instantaneously whizzed past. We encountered a large
group of Fox hounds. They were so powerful that I will
never forget the force that passed us that day. We
certainly did not want to get in their way. They were
wired, clearly on a mission and Dexter and I were so
lucky to come out unscathed. I recall the hunting
hounds' spots (large tri colour blocks) of colour
galloping past, accompanied by the most horrendous
barking and baying.

A short car ride away from our home, there is an
option of a starting point for walks, parking at the local
pub or farm. On one occasion, Dexter and I parked up
and when I opened the boot of the car for Dexter to get
out, I was astonished when another male liver spotted
Dalmatian and a little Westie dog ran up to the car,
jumped in and joined Dexter! The owner rushed over
and was very apologetic. Dexter didn't mind, all three of
the clan were sitting comfortably in the back. When I
chatted further to the owner of this Dalmatian called
Lucky, who lived at a nearby farm, we were both
impressed to hear that Dexter and Lucky were actually
brothers. It then all clicked into place why on several
occasions taking this particular walk people had
mistaken Lucky for Dexter and vice versa – they truly
were both handsome, lovely and gentle liver spotted
boys, albeit Dexter was taller and Lucky in fact was a

year older. Again, you've guessed it ….Trouble was their father and my, what a busy boy he had been!

More confusion often arose when walking in and around our village. We discovered that there was another Dalmatian, also called Dexter, would you believe. He was a big black spotted male, not liver spotted like Dexter and for once was totally unrelated to our boy. This Dexter unfortunately had a bit of a reputation, so we quickly learned to point out that our Dexter quite obviously had different colour spots and that these two boys were entirely different characters altogether. People could be so rude and ignorant insisting that my dog had attacked. This was most upsetting especially as my Dexter's behaviour was exemplary; he had done absolutely nothing wrong. I must add that we never once encountered any problems with "the other Dexter". Our Dexter got along with others famously – he never judged, was calm, respectful and balanced in nature and this was reflected back in his relationships and popularity stakes for sure.

Daily walks are essential for dogs and also life-enhancing for dog owners too. Dexter and I enjoyed so many different and varied walks in the local and surrounding areas. We feel very lucky to live where we do and to be able to enjoy nature on our doorstep, especially all the wonderful wildlife. It's very easy to get caught up in the perpetual motion of work, decisions, and events and so on that make up our lives. Dexter ensured that we were motivated to take time out for walks.

Dexter was a gentle soul and ever so loved by all creatures' great and small. Dexter was endlessly tolerant. He offered children something very special indeed, by empathetically helping them with social and emotional interaction, including those who had previously had adverse reaction. For some of the local kids walking home from school, if Dexter was out and about, it was the highlight of their day. Dexter particularly loved to have my nieces and nephews stay at our home. Dexter snuggled his way into quite literally everyone's hearts. Dexter meant so much, to so many people. Dexter was such a great dog that he happily shared his environment with all animal and human friends that visited and came to stay. Food, treats, toys and of course love were shared. He was totally and utterly selfless. Dexter's mentality was very much 'the more, the merrier'. We often looked after friends and neighbours animals (one Labrador dog I recall even stayed for six weeks whilst the family holidayed). Dexter was so accommodating and we did our utmost to make our guests feel at home. No-one ever wanted to leave.

A Peacock, who we affectionately called Percy, surprisingly landed in our garden one day. He took up residence and was a friendly character with only one eye. For three weeks Percy enjoyed alternating between both ours and our immediate next door neighbour's garden.

We fed crackers, daily at our doorstep to Percy. Dexter was never jealous and happily shared. The experience was rather surreal. I remember Dexter on one occasion when he was older, finding two tiny newborn, orphaned field mice under the hedgerow of our back garden. Sadly, one mouse was dead and the other looked fragile to say the least. Strangely, Dexter began licking the tiny mouse. It was an attempt to warm and revive him. Dexter then looked at Richard and me as if summoning our assistance and how could we ignore his plea. We as human beings have a responsibility to care for wildlife too.

We took the tiny fellow inside and made him a snug bed in a little pet carrier and then popped him in the airing cupboard to warm him up. It worked; he didn't look nearly as blue and cold. Under Dexter's watchful eye I prepared some warmed rice milk and fed the little baby orphan mouse from a pipette every few hours or so, Dexter would always remind me when he needed a feed. The little orphan was small and fragile. I picked him up each time on a cotton wool pad and we cleaned his tiny bottom with cotton wool buds as a substitute for the cleaning that he would receive from his mother. My family and friends thought I was mad, even though they know I will do absolutely anything to help an animal in need.

Nevertheless, when I rang our local RSPCA wildlife section to check if we were caring for him appropriately, the guy taking the call was amazed. He asked initially what colour fur the baby mouse had when Dexter found him. When I replied pink (no fur) there was a long silence on the end of the telephone. I continued to give a description, size, the fact that he hadn't yet opened his eyes, ears were forming; he hadn't yet managed to walk but was indeed starting to wobble, move about a bit and so on. Finally, I heard a chuckle and a reply on the line to carry on what we (Dexter and I) were doing as we were certainly doing a marvellous job. He added that the RSPCA could do no more so we shouldn't take him in. Dexter and I cared for that little mouse with love and tenderness. Everything I did for him was carefully supervised by Dexter and we became very fond of him indeed. As he was tiny and pink my nephew, Tom, named him "little Willy" which amused us all enormously!

After almost a fortnight, sadly little Willy passed away most unexpectedly. He was getting much bigger and stronger and both Dexter and I were very shocked and upset to say the least. He had been doing so well and we all had high hopes for him to become strong enough to be released back into nature but despite all that we did sadly, it was not to be. We tried our very best to help him but we couldn't raise him as his mother could. We buried him in a wooden box, next to Oliver, our lovely little hamster who had passed away, over a decade ago.. We loved Oliver, he was a super little character and lived to a ripe and vigorous old age. Oliver and little Willy had a lovely, peaceful resting place in our back garden, under the beautiful mature trees.

Just like we mourned Oliver's passing, Dexter grieved following the loss of his little mouse. Our vet commented how he had only ever encountered female dogs behaving in such a gentle, nurturing manner. It was truly remarkable. Dexter was very sensitive and such a sweet, caring soul. Dexter easily made friends with all humans and animals alike. He made people smile and could melt the hardest of hearts. Dexter showed me that gentleness is indeed a great strength.

"Thursday 16th June

Chaos today at the Country Park! I've discovered that the usually brilliantly behaved Dexter gets a wee bit over-excited in the company of his adolescent sister! Little monkeys... they decided to make their own fun, instead of chasing the ball. All revved up, they did a swift, ever so slight detour and hijacked a nearby picnic. I nearly died of embarrassment! Their 'paw-fect steal' actually turned out to be an empty crisp packet so all was well but what a letdown for the flamboyant performers! Hopefully this will discourage ANY further possible temptation!? :~"

5

DEXTER'S ADVENTURES

Prior to having Dexter, Richard and I had worked hard throughout all our annual holiday leave entitlements to renovate our home. We had not had a holiday for some years. Dexter was still a youngster, not even a year old when we decided that it might be nice to have a long weekend all together and enjoy some more of the British countryside... and where better than the Lake District. We did some research and found a dog friendly inn to stay at. There are so many places now that pets are welcome which is fabulous and very encouraging.

We packed the car, our clothes and Dexter's bed, food, toys and off we trotted. Dexter was a great traveller – nothing phased him and the journey was enjoyable with so much beautiful scenery to take in. When we arrived at our destination we were greeted with a warm welcome and soon settled into our lovely, homely room.

It was a real treat to enjoy a break, all of us together. The food was delicious; there was no internet connection or mobile telephones, (no mobile signal) and such lovely scenery and surroundings. Dexter went for a nap in our room whilst we ate dinner. We thought he would appreciate the comfort of his own cosy bed and benefit from a good sound sleep after his walk, without the distraction and temptation of the glorious food being served up. We understand that Dexter did enjoy a rest but chose an alternative resting place for relaxation ...well, so the maid discovered when she let herself in to our room.

Dexter for the first time ever, had climbed up on to our bed and was clearly enjoying a restful, relaxing snooze stretching out. Only raising his head and wagging his tail to observe the maid placing clean towels, flannels, soaps and chocolates to each side of him. It was in fact the maid's first day at the inn and she was from New Zealand. She actually had no idea that this was a "dog friendly" place so was completely stunned when she saw Dexter relaxing, stretched out across the bed. Nevertheless, she diligently carried out her duties, perplexed as she was. She was later heard many times, chuckling and telling everyone "well, I guessed he was friendly as his tail was bat, bat, batting on the bed". Ooops! He really shouldn't have been on the human's bed but it was so funny hearing her recount her tale and especially hearing her excited tone and accent. Thankfully, no-one appeared to mind and we were most relieved that he didn't eat the chocolates or soaps either. Bless him; he was still young after all.

We had a truly great time away, enjoying glorious weather, scenery and walks galore. Dexter had shown us that we needed and deserved this short break. It was appreciated and advantageous to us all. Dexter was a dream, such a good boy, even at that young age walking through fields and farms full of distractions and count- less sheep. He never once chased or attempted to make chase, choosing to stay beside us, always positively rewarded for his exemplary behaviour. Please don't be confused into thinking that I am advocating off-leash walking around sheep or other livestock, a long loose line is a sensible option. A little treat of locally produced sausages was a firm favourite and after all, Dexter could not be expected to visit the Lake District without sampling the highly sought after local Cumberland sausage.

Although we had maps to guide us on our walks, we seldom referred to them since our beloved little "Snout Nav" as we had already affectionately nicknamed him, always made sure we were on the right track. Remark- able really, and thank heavens because I'm certainly no map reader! We brought back home a souvenir from this trip in the form on an unwanted host - Dexter had picked up a tick. A Spot On formula had been prescribed by the vet before we went away to treat some little spots that had appeared under the skin on his head (you can be forgiven for thinking that was a typo reading about a Dalmatian with spots!). However, the particular Spot On formula that was administered, did not provide cover for ticks, only fleas, mites etc so please let that serve as a reminder to thoroughly check what you are protecting your animals against. In the myriad of solutions and potions, I appreciate this is really difficult especially when given or administered by your veterinary practice and you have not read the necessary information yourself.

The spots incidentally, after several courses of treatment, were found to be Dally Rash. I handed my book to the vets and asked for their guidance and advise, having learned of this through re-reading one of the Dalmatian handbooks that I had purchased before Dexter's arrival. Further investigation was carried out in the form of a skin scrape. Dalmatian owners please look out - forewarned is forearmed to get the appropriate treatment.

We were told that the underlying cause for Dally Rash is usually the Demodex mite which lives in the hair follicle. The mite is apparently passed from mum to pup after birth and can be extremely tricky to eradicate. The book advises that it is normally present in small numbers but if the numbers increase, the immune system can no longer deal with the situation. This sudden increase or imbalance can be brought on by many causes including stress and sometimes even something like a small, simple cut or scratch in the area. Spring and summer are the most common times for the outbreaks which is when this happened to Dexter. Thank goodness we sought prompt veterinary treatment and caught this in the very early stages. Parasites can be extremely detrimental to a pet's wellbeing.

We enjoyed ourselves so much on holiday. So, a few weeks later we decided to go camping with my dearest friend Sarah and her boyfriend at the time. That was an experience I can tell you ... a busy bank holiday weekend on Anglesey, North Wales. Every morning as we unzipped our little tent, we were excitedly greeted by what can only be assumed to be every single child staying on the campsite that weekend to the chorus of "Dalmatian, Dalmatian". Our Dexter certainly was admired and adored and there always seemed to be a chorus of 101 comments (please excuse the pun but we heard them all) everywhere he went. People always seem to notice a Dalmatian, especially little people! Children, including those not old enough to talk, seemingly even attempt to pronounce "Dalmatian".

This campsite was packed out and all the tents were crammed in like sardines, I think the site owners were cashing in and making the most of the decent bank holiday weather. None of us got much sleep that weekend as you could hear many a conversation, dogs barking etc from neighbouring tents. Dexter didn't mind, in fact he loved it! He was really well behaved and very much enjoyed his celebrity status on the campsite. Dex really should have had a star on the campsite walk of fame. We all enjoyed the beach walks, the sea air and the company. Unfortunately, Sarah was poorly following a recent overseas visit, despite having had all the necessary travel vaccinations. She was so ill; she had to return home early from our break which was a shame as the weather was amazing for a bank holiday. We promised there would be more holidays and weekends away to come. Dexter was, after all a seasoned traveller now.

Vaccinations are also important for our animals. They are key to ensuring our pets are protected against the common transmutable diseases, many of them lethal to dogs. Dexter was a sensitive soul though and unfortunately reacted adversely to vaccinations. On one occasion following his annual booster, the injection site erupted with a tennis ball size lump or abscess and Homeopathic medicine thankfully assisted to negate the undesirable effects in this particular instance. It is very difficult when people and their pets are sensitive to routine, conventional medications, especially if you are unaware that there are other solutions or remedies that can work in place of, or in conjunction with to assist.

Nowadays, dogs in the UK do not always need a "full" vaccination every year as was previously the recommendation. There is evidence that the distemper, parvo and hepatitis parts will last for three years, if a dog receives at least two puppy vaccinations and then a booster a year later. You can check your own dog's level of cover for immunity/antibodies present if you are concerned about over vaccinating your dog by blood titre testing them. The Leptospirosis component (which is now a separate vaccination not core) however, differs from the others in that laboratory testing shows a short duration of immunity. Annual lepto is now recommended but can also be titre tested too. Leptospirosis cover is also really important as it is common in the UK since it is spread via the urine of rodents, wildlife and farm animals, either directly or via contaminated food or water. So, this may be required if your dog swims and is out and about enjoying walks in the countryside. If you are at all concerned about vaccines do talk to your vet, as many are now embracing titre testing methods which may help you make the best decision for your dog.

With suitable, preventative measures in place to repel and protect against the possible transmission of infection from ticks and other nasties, we continued on our next trip away to Scotland. This was to Richard's cousins wedding in Ullapool (North West Scotland). We hired a motor home for the duration so that we could take Dexter along with us and also enjoy the long journey in comfort, making various overnight stops. We took our time and very much enjoyed the experience, stopping for breaks to stretch our legs. Taking in the sights and sounds along the way was fun and interesting. However, as we got closer to our destination the weather took a turn for the worse. We took our overnight stop as we

JOANNE JARVIS

planned but when we opened the curtains in the morning we were literally buried beneath the night's snow fall.

What a beautiful sight, but boy it was cold. Everything was frozen solid. We wrapped up and took a walk into the village to buy a heat lamp to defrost all our pipes and were absolutely amazed by just how much snow had fallen. Dexter was so excited and bounded through the fresh snow excitedly catching snowballs and then looking curiously when they magically disappeared. What fun we were having, but we did have a wedding to go to. Richard ended up literally shovelling tonnes of snow to make two tracks long enough to reach the main road from the campsite. Dexter was more than willing to help dig too and finally we were on our way again.

We made it to our destination in good time for the wedding. Dexter came along to the ceremony as it was held outside, in an arboretum. Dexter was brilliantly behaved and thoroughly enjoyed the music and company of a little Spanish waterdog guest and human guests alike at the ceillidh (particularly the young man with the rabbit skin sporran which he sniffed enthusiastically)! Hmm. It was seriously cold in Scotland, so cold in fact that I had to wrap little Dexter up in the motor caravan especially at night. I gave him a covered hot water bottle too. He certainly never objected and appreciated snuggling up to it, but it was a little while yet before we were to discover why this was the case and why he found it beneficial.

We purchased a little old caravan the following summer after enjoying this trip. Dexter, Richard and I had all enjoyed our time away and as nice as it was to have spent time in accommodation previously, our little caravan served as a home from home, just waiting to be hooked up to go wherever, and whenever we could. Dexter and Richard particularly loved the freedom the open road gave us. Over time, we eventually upgraded to a motor home which made things even easier and was more comfortable for travel for us all too. We loved the great outdoors, just sitting chatting and taking the time and opportunity to appreciate a rest. Dexter especially loved supervising barbeques. Even with such temptation, he was so well behaved we rarely put him on a lead on the caravan sites. He always stayed close to us.

We enjoyed many trips to the Lake District, Yorkshire, Derbyshire, Wales, and Scotland. We saw many spectacular sights and scenery and we made lots of friends along the way. One particular encounter springs to mind. Writing and recalling this makes my heart fill with pride. I look back and remember as if it were yesterday, that we were wandering through the bustling seaside town of Aberystwyth. Dexter was thoroughly enjoying the sights and smells. As usual he stopped to say hello to everyone who greeted him. Dexter loved absolutely everyone, no matter what their race, age, sex or status. I will never forget the whole of my life the gratitude a homeless man showed us for allowing him to smooth and make a fuss of our lovely Dexter. No-one had acknowledged the man the whole day, not even for a good morning or good afternoon or even a look his way. So the joy that came from the outpouring of the unconditional love, licks and wags from Dexter was truly overwhelming for this chap.

Dexter's great love enriched our lives and the lives of so many. He made friends wherever he went and demonstrated that we, as humans are not the only beings motivated by feelings of concern and compassion for others. Healing comes in many forms and watching the effect animals have on humans is most humbling. Dexter was a joy to be with and reminded us to always make the best of life whatever the circumstances.

Throughout our trips, he was always accommodating and easy going. Content to explore any environment, in any setting. He very much appreciated and thoroughly enjoyed all of his adventures. We visited many different villages, towns, and cities, affluent areas and those not so. Dexter cherished his family and valued his home and surrounding areas too. So long as we were together, wherever we were, that was all that mattered. Every day was an adventure in Dexter's book.

"Tuesday 2nd March
Me, Rich and Dex nearly ended up on an upcoming episode of Coronation Street! Travelling home from Chatsworth House, we stopped to stretch our legs in the Derbyshire countryside. Ended up watching Corrie, on location ... the filming of a car crash scene (just finishing up).

Dexter helped clear up food scraps dropped near the butty van. He was un-fazed by such an entourage, the hustle and bustle, the lighting and emergency vehicles. This was one hell of a 'mock' incident. Made me think about Rich, being in the Fire Service and doing extrication like this in real life.

Dexter was a super-star even though he wasn't caught on camera ."

6

CHANGE

Many of us work tremendously hard to give ourselves a better life. My career accomplishments had been very gratifying before I had to give up my job due to illness. This was not an immediate transition I have to say, but we do not often recognise the signs, and struggle on until it is too late – don't we?! Following an accident I could not even drive into work let alone perform my duties and actually work. Rather than rest and attempt to recover as advised (hindsight is a wonderful thing, I know), I struggled on in agony to work from home in an attempt to keep my job going. Yes, I had burnt the candle at both ends, but I thought I was indestructible. Having had operations previously I had always recovered quickly and returned to work in record time.

I very much enjoyed my job, working for the company for many years, and had recently been promoted. I did not want to take time off work, I had always been of the mindset to stride on through life and put up with things. Ironically, we are constantly busy despite having things such as computers and labour saving devices to generate efficiency and effectiveness these days. Life is demanding and our little world time really had been whizzing along at hyper speed. It was my orthopaedic surgeon who knew me well, that finally switched on the light that made me see that I was never going to recover and be able to carry on as I had done previously. In fact things would worsen if I continued as I was doing. A complete life style change was in order and it seemed that any plans for a fulfilling, energetic work-life balance might be scuppered.

Dexter was by my side always helping me. He was my strength and motivation and gave me companionship and unconditional love. He seemingly adjusted his step to mine and helped me to understand that it is such trials, events and circumstances that enable us to evaluate who we really are and in turn provide us with a greater appreciation of life and what matters most to us. Slowing down helped me to manage my condition, listen and truly observe and appreciate the simple things in life. Without Dexter I honestly do not know where I would be now. I never felt lonely or bored as one might expect giving up my job and stopping everything, not knowing what my purpose may be next. I took responsibility for my own health and found it was impossible to be frustrated by restriction or become down or depressed with Dexter around. I was as devoted to him as he was to me, we were an inseparable duo. We enjoyed the most gentle of walks together. I found that slowing down both physically and mentally, not being glued to the phone, on the computer or in meetings all day, heightened my senses to the natural world.

Dexter would enjoy taking his time sniffing. We no longer rushed. Standing silently in the fields day by day, we watched wildlife, nature and the ongoing cycles of change. The colours and landscape as strange as it may sound were somewhat previously outside of my radar. Most likely because I was always so busy running around day in, day out and didn't pay much attention to my surrounding or make the time to look around. I had not been aware of such subtle changes, happening every day with the trees and flowers, for example. I hadn't appreciated these simple joys of being outside.

Perhaps it is only when we are still long enough to absorb everything that's going on around us and in our lives, that we begin to notice such things. Slowing down, spending time with Dexter and respectfully observing our world increased focus, self awareness and opened doors of wonder and wisdom for me. To have time to yourself, especially out in nature, is one of the best things and to know what matters and what does not, is some-thing that we all may benefit from. Lives are so busy these days; everything is twenty-four-seven. It's a whirlwind.

It was around this time that I sensed something was not right with Dexter too. Yes he'd had some bad luck but both of us were now creaking, cracking, misaligned and unpredictably limping. I felt like a doddery old lady and Dexter no longer leapt and bounded as he should. I've heard it said that a dog chooses you (not the other way round) and animals sometimes mirror us both phys- ically and emotionally. I had heard of animals and their owners both diagnosed with similar health problems but this was crazy. Dexter was still a young dog.

He showed me that he could no longer even jump in and out of the car and we had recently purchased a ramp to assist him. Our beautiful boy had sadly sustained an injury a short while ago when a friend's dog had boister- ously dived on his back and floored him for no apparent reason other than her pretentious dominance. She was a strong and powerful hunting breed and clearly had inherent predatory instincts. We were on her patch that day. In the past, we had walked with her, on neutral territory without any issue.

Dexter's screams and howls of agony will haunt me till the very day I die. I am sorry to say that I saw the awful incident happening in the blink of an eye. And it was so distressing especially as our lovely lad was just calmly walking along at that time, unsuspectingly watching the swans swimming gracefully across the lake. There was nothing I or anyone else for that matter could do - it all happened so quickly. He was left flattened with his back right leg in an extremely peculiar position out to one side. I wished I could have kept him safe as I struggled to help him up.

As much as I have tried to forget and let go of the sorrow associated with this incident, it is ingrained in my memory. This particular friend is a responsible dog owner and she did everything she could to understand and control her powerful breed of dog at that time. Reading lots of books and enlisting the help of a qualified behaviourist, after an incident with a jogger that followed. She learnt a lot because of her dog and subsequently has a lovely crossbreed rescue dog, which has without a doubt benefited from all the knowledge gained. This serves to identify, and for us all to remember, how potentially dangerous any animal can be and even more so without appropriate handling, training, stimulation, proper care and attention that every animal deserves.

Having a dog is a very precious experience. I realise that we are not the only ones to encounter the pain and devastation of seeing an accident or attack. Understandably, the trauma is often hard to forget. The injury Dexter sustained during this incident severely damaged his back right leg and caused misalignment, discomfort, pain and tension throughout his entire body. We never walked with her again and kept our distance. Unbeknown to us, we were soon to discover the reason why this incident caused so much pain and suffering.

We tried pain killers, nutritional supplements, weeks of rest, courses of osteopathy and hydrotherapy but there was little improvement. Dexter had begun to act old beyond his years. He was in pain and it was breaking my heart. We were extra vigilant going out for short walks, but sometimes we would come across other dog owners that could be most insensitive and intolerant. Playful, unruly and boisterous dogs would bound up and "he/she only wants to play" would be shouted from a distance which was of little help. It is hard for responsible people, attempting to keep their animals safe, when someone else's dog is out of control and making what could have been a peaceful, enjoyable, tranquil walk very difficult. Essentially causing discomfort, some of the dog owners on our walks appeared so engrossed with their mobile phones that they didn't notice, or care, that their dog was jumping up and on occasions even knocking Dexter over, resulting in further setbacks.

We as animal owners, rely heavily on the expertise of trusted veterinarians. However, the veterinary practice we were registered with, I am sad to say, were unfortunately of little help or assistance at this time. We were told that X-rays showed nothing. Poor Dexter had already picked up kennel cough from their surgery when he was back and forth having bandages changed over prolonged periods, after undergoing several procedures for a cut paw when he was younger. He hadn't been able to mix with other dogs during this time as he was only permitted to have lead walks. A dog was coughing in the waiting room on one of our visits to the surgery. The dog should have been isolated and was after I queried it with a receptionist. By then of course it was too late.

Anyone whose dog has picked up a nasty kennel cough infection will know how terrible and troublesome it is. Many people inoculate their animals against kennel cough, especially if they will regularly be going into kennels. Dexter was never once kennelled so we never inoculated him for this as he always holidayed with us. These vaccines are given as drops (nasal spray) and we were told that they are not 100% effective because a dog can still get kennel cough from another virus source or bacteria despite vaccination. Therefore, we tried to limit the amount of chemicals in his individual case and circumstances since we did not want to overload Dexter's system with what we perceived to be possibly unnecessary drugs. In hindsight, perhaps if we had inoculated him, he might have been spared the treatment needed to clear the infection.

With regard to the cut paw, to make matters worse, during one visit to the vets, it was bandaged inappropriately. Subsequently, our lovely Dexter was subjected to surgery and further antibiotics to prevent infection. This went on for months and months. The removal of the dew claw was necessary as the ligaments were damaged as a result of bandages being fitted too tight and it had to be removed as the poor fellow would only have to pick up a toy or knock it with his other front leg and the dew claw would stick out precariously, bleed and cause pain. Incidentally the cut itself had to be tackled twice under surgery as initially it did not heal. Dexter never grumbled even with all the hindrance, pain and drama of this. He was wonderful. He was patient, trusting and brave – never needing an Elizabethan collar (pet lamp-shade) to deter him from tampering with the bandages.

All of the problems that we encountered were a huge blow. We had put blind trust in this veterinary practice. To be told that Dexter's hips and joints were "fine" wasn't good enough. There were clearly multiple problems here. Dexter was in pain, and getting worse, why couldn't they see? I was with him most of the time and could only see deterioration not improvement. This wasn't right at all. Someone had to help him. If only we knew that referrals to Supervet, Noel Fitzpatrick were available at this time. Sadly, this was before this amazing man appeared on television and many years before his world leading centre was opened. We had no idea that he practiced.

Consequently we researched and changed vets and were fortunate enough to be under the care of a respected, knowledgeable, orthopaedic vet who treated Dexter with care and compassion. This lovely Irish vet conducted an extremely thorough examination actually watching Dexter on the surgery car park, move through his paces (something that had not been done before) and really listened when we talked through how his health had deteriorated. Finally, after further thorough and necessary x-rays/scans, since the multitude of previous costly x-rays at the previous vets practice proved worthless, we heard the dreaded news.

Dexter was a very poorly lad indeed. Suffering from a very aggressive Spondylosis of the spine for which there was no cure, we were also informed that he had various other spine, joint and ligament problems too. No wonder he howled in absolute agony when he was floored by my friend's dog. But all that was in the past, over and done with and sadly cannot be changed. Dexter never held grudges or held on to painful memories like you or I might.

Spondylosis in dogs, the vet explained is said to be a reasonably common condition of the bones that is seen among older dogs and this needed to be managed with painkillers as heartbreakingly, no surgery could be done to cure Dexter at this time. Spondylosis is known as the disease which causes the dog's vertebrae to begin to grow together. Spondylosis is found to be a progressive condition and can affect a dog's life in a fairly major way since nerves can be affected as a result of fusing bone. Most Spondylosis in dogs occurs in the later years of their lives and very few have very long to live and therefore a relatively short amount of time to suffer. Clearly, this was not the case with Dexter.

We were always mindful that the enormous rate of growth that large breed puppies experience does put them at risk for bone and joint problems in later life. However, Dexter was still only a relatively young dog and we were absolutely devastated learning of all his health problems. Nevertheless, we picked ourselves up and took full responsibility for Dexter's care. I explored and investigated many different avenues including a holistic approach in the hope of alleviating pain and discomfort. Under the watchful eye of our supportive vet, we spent a fortune on supplements and enzymes. We tried anything available to complement his conventional drugs and treatment. We literally did everything that we could to help him, nurture him, understand his condition and make him as comfortable as possible. Having Dexter was such a privilege, he was extra special and our bond had taught me to trust my feelings and intuition. We were quite right to change to another veterinary practice - and to nurture and treat animals with the respect and compassion that our beloved companions deserve.

Dexter was a true example of perseverance and determination. Although he needed daily medication to manage any pain and discomfort, routine hydrotherapy to strengthen muscles and limit stiffness, he taught us to also look past physical problems and limitations. As a result of such we adapted his environment and approached tasks, games, outings and things differently and successfully so he could still participate in activities and continue to go on outings, meet people and other animal friends as he so loved.

Although it was upsetting to do so, we responsibly contacted the Dalmatian breeder, since there was a possibility that some of his problems could have been hereditary. We had chosen a reputable breeder that promoted good breeding practice, whether or not this was genetic or just bad luck, we were dismayed to hear her ask if we were ringing to ask for money back. Nothing could have been further from the truth. We didn't want money, we just wanted to alert her and to prevent such an occurrence from happening again, to spare the suffering of other animals and upset to their owners and guardians. Sadly we later discovered that Dexter's half sister also suffered from a condition of the spine too.

I do not condemn reputable breeders as they conscientiously try to raise puppies from good genetic lines and they should not be confused with Puppy farms. Puppy farmers are irresponsible and breed puppies for profit, with little or no regard for the health and welfare of the puppies or their parents. Thank heavens legislation will soon be in force to stamp out unscrupulous people who ultimately can cause lifelong problems for dogs. The dedicated orthopaedic vet who diagnosed Dexter's health problems sadly moved on to practice over in Ireland and unfortunately the veterinary practice was subsequently merged with a large corporate. This trusted orthopaedic vet at this practice had told us absolutely nothing could be done to save Dexter, surgery, drugs or otherwise, yet the new staff were constantly pestering to have him scanned, poked and prodded. I did not want to put him under more anaesthetic unnecessarily. Dexter had pain relieving medications and been given a diagnosis after all. Additional scans would not make him better, alter the treatment and could in fact actually make him temporarily feel worse. I had discovered from our vet that animals (during x-rays), had to be stretched and moved into unnatural positions for the x-rays and scans to be completed. Such positions were obviously essential to enable a diagnosis to be made, but when not under anaesthetic these positions would have been uncomfortable for some animals with problems like Dexter's to achieve, thus resulting in yet further possible pain and stiffness after the procedure has taken place. There have been technological advancements since then!

We fully understand that x-ray's and scans are absolutely imperative in detecting and diagnosing health conditions and also determining how treatment is progressing, but for Dexter there was no cure at this time. Dexter had been given his diagnosis after his multitudinous x-rays and we were assured by the vet that Dexter certainly did not need further scans to determine how his condition was progressing. The vet told us that we would be able to see that for ourselves. We strived to keep pain to an absolute minimum and do what was morally correct for Dexter as an individual in his own right - so long as he was happy, comfortable and had a good quality of life that was all that mattered.

Sadly it has to be said that some veterinary practices these days (not all thankfully) appear to have a great deal of focus on monetary gain. In our experience, exploitation of pet insurance and commercial connection with pet food companies can sometimes appear more important than the animals in their care. Wouldn't it be wonderful if all veterinary practices were like Noel Fitzpatrick's centres of excellence? The focus clearly being on prevention, diagnosis and treatment for animals. Noel is super talented, dedicated, and authentic and speaks our language. I have attended 'Dog fest' and listened intently to him as a speaker. The work that he passionately initiates and that he and his fabulous team carry out is world-leading and instrumental in improving the lives of animals and humans alike.

It was because of our experiences and Dexter's sensitivities that I searched and sought the help of a vet, qualified in both homeopathy and conventional medicine. Dexter was taking conventional medications to remove the pain of his condition, which enabled him to keep moving unaided and maintain quality of life, but he was experiencing side effects. The homeopathy worked in conjunction and served to lessen some of them. Despite following a complete food diet recommended by the previous veterinary practice, Dexter had lots of additional health problems related to infected anal glands. Because of his spinal condition he could not express his glands by scooting along the floor or ground as other dogs might do. The conventional vet we were consulting with prior to this, wanted to remove his anal glands which we did not want her to do. After lots of research and a better understanding of food for canines, I introduced him to a holistic nutritious diet. With our new vet's assistance and prescribed remedies, combined with the holistic diet and supplements, Dexter never suffered from this problem again and more importantly, many of the side effects from the pain killing conventional medications were also alleviated, as we had hoped.

We were so lucky to find Mike who is extremely knowledgeable, compassionate, respected and such a good, honest and amazing vet. Qualified and working for many years in both the fields of homeopathy and conventional medicine. He was, and is, always there when we need him. He is sadly soon to retire from consulting in the surgery but available to offer advice on the end of the telephone. Mike has always had the best interest of the animals under his care at heart. In my opinion, both conventional and complimentary go hand in hand. I'm not a sticker and am pretty open minded. I have a foot in both camps and understand that when one is desperate to be out of pain (as so many of us sadly know) one really will try anything.

I'm not sure I should divulge the story about when Dexter had licked the miniscule remains of cake mixture from the 'special carrot cake' bowl. I had rinsed the mixing bowl (obviously not very well) and loaded it in the lower drawer of the dishwasher. I realise some people will judge me for trialling 'alternatives' after I had to stop taking prescribed medication for pain having had an adverse reaction. I did perhaps eat too much, I admit that. It was nice carrot cake. Consequently, I did not experiment again. Dosage was too difficult to judge and I am clearly very sensitive (not an experience I want to repeat)! However, I will say that I slept well, appeared to experience reduction in pain levels and I positively floated about. Dexter looked after me and did not leave my side, bless him. A remarkable experiment, but all too risky to repeat and I am super thankful that Dexter did not suffer any adverse reaction.

I add that Cannabidoil (CBD) which is a natural occurring compound found in the flower of cannabis is now legal to possess, buy and sell in the UK, providing the product doesn't not contain more than 0.3% THC. Both CBD and THC are reported to have therapeutic attributes for both animals and humans. There is anecdotal evidence suggesting it can help treat pain, as well as controlling seizures.

Sadly, around this time my lovely mum was diagnosed with cancer and also endured a series of strokes. First mini strokes, then the first major one leaving her with aphasia (communication and understanding difficulties). This was doubly heartbreaking to see. These were emotionally and physically wrenching times for us all. We had to be stronger than I ever could have thought. I felt so tired, in a lot of pain myself because of my illness and exhausted by family tragedies. We really were pushed to our emotional and physical limits. Everything felt a challenge, even a short walk, but we persevered. These trials and events shaped and built our characters for sure. I walked with a hiking pole at his time, which helped both me and Dexter, as degenerative changes progressed. It also served to block and prevent unruly animals from getting too close to our precious boy. Just by planting the pole onto the ground, a seemingly invisible boundary was established which discouraged unwanted advances.

We philosophically accepted our lot, kept going and carried on smiling ...the power of human nature is a driving force for sure. I devoted myself to those around me, and Dexter made sure we didn't take life too seriously. Looking back, the fact that I was around, albeit not being able to do any enormous amount physically myself, I spent much time sitting with Mum and Dexter and appreciating their company. I am sure this made all the difference to Mum especially as she could no longer communicate over the telephone. Sometimes a simple act of kindness, a caring action, and tone of voice, your expression, energy, a smile or a small gesture can be very meaningful to someone with communication or physical difficulties. Through acting as a bridge between worlds, we can experience deep connection, even picking up emotions and thoughts of others, not just of people but animals too.

" Sunday 27th May

Dexter's first Hydrotherapy session was brilliant. Great to see him safely stretch out and swim so elegantly! No restriction turning, the pool is human sized and he can get in and out himself when he wants a rest. Might not need the buoyancy aid when he gets a bit stronger. Rich was wanting to get in with him, it's such a beautiful pool! Perfect low impact exercise. Dex clearly loves it, and he gets to take his fav mini football along too. One VERY happy boy ."

7

HOME COMFORTS

I would have done anything for Dexter. My physical and emotional pain were less important than his welfare; and learning of his health problems made him even more extra special and precious to me. It became my mission to make Dexter's life as comfortable as possible especially as his condition would only worsen. Whatever adaptations we could do to help Dexter, we did them – anything within our means that he needed we purchased. We listened attentively to the experts and specialists we consulted and were encouraged to find we had already introduced some of the recommended aids and adaptations.

Richard and I had a special bond with Dexter and he had shown us much of what he needed. He already had the ramp to assist getting in and out of the car. He had numerous well made suitable coats and fleece jumpers to keep him and his major organs warm and prevent his muscles from going into spasm and from stiffness setting in. The Orthopaedic Vet had told us he must always be kept warm. We took Dexter for hydrotherapy sessions routinely – he had a special fleece suit to wear once he was dried off, this further removed moisture from his coat and kept him warm and comfortable.

We gave him conventional medications, complementary therapies and supplements and he enjoyed a varied, nutritious and wholesome diet of home cooked and holistic food. Different dogs require different nutrients. Just like humans, no two dogs are ever the same. Dexter had nutritional requirements because of his medical condition. Fortunately, he did not need a special diet low in 'purines' as he did not have urinary tract problems which the Dalmatian breed is rather prone to. All the changes that we made did indeed help. He even had a therapeutic magnetic collar. Everything combined reduced the need for high doses of conventional drugs. We tried so hard to ensure he always had what he needed and tried anything that might help him. Dexter was so loved and people would often remark that he was lucky to have owners like us, but we were the lucky ones for sure. Bowls were raised to a more comfortable height for feeding. Little things like this make such a big difference to a pet with difficulties. I must add here that food was one of Dexter's greatest loves – he always had an insatiable appetite so no bowl was raised for any amount of time! He was always brilliant taking medications especially if disguised in salmon mousse or natural recipe wet food.

Downstairs we originally had wooden floors in our home, but had carpets fitted on top of them to prevent Dexter from accidentally slipping and falling as he was sometimes unpredictably unsteady, especially when rising or getting out of his bed. The thick underlay and cosy carpet proved invaluable and was most comfortable for him to lie and stretch out on as and when he needed. As carpets were not laid in the kitchen big rugs were strategically placed to make life easier for him and to assist him, especially when getting out of bed. It all helped and made our home a lot warmer, also keeping the central heating on a low constant heat and the lounge log burner stoked up in the cooler months too. We were told he must never be allowed to get cold and he most certainly did not.

We took each day as it came, adapting walking accordingly. We struggled on and made the most of each day but also getting the rest we both needed. This helped enormously as Dexter's condition developed, and also for my own health condition, giving me the energy and strength for visiting my dear mum who was in hospital for many months at a time. Mum was amazing, so strong and so too, was our dear, courageous, Dexter. Assisting and observing both mum and Dexter quietly enabled me to see what was needed, what was helping and what wasn't. For example Dexter would often put big soft toys under his chin making us see that he needed support from something like a pillow to align his neck and make a comfortable resting position when lying down.

When he was comfortable and settled, Dexter would sleep blissfully for hours. After much research we purchased amazing beds for him with bolstered sides (just the right size and height for him to attain this comfortable position unaided). I have to say the beds were enormous; made of thick luxurious and supportive memory foam. Dexter absolutely loved them and they made a world of difference to him and his quality of sleep. One bed was so big we had to remove a kitchen cupboard for it to be housed – people thought we were mad going to such extremes, but if it helped, we really would do anything to make him comfortable. This bed fitted perfectly in our motor home so Dexter always had the benefit of a comfortable bed. The company who manufacture these beautiful beds in America make them to last forever. In the scheme of things I was so sad this was not going to be the case for our darling Dexter. How I wished he'd had one of these sooner. Truly I had a heartfelt desire to help any way that was possible.

We designed and purpose-made a memory foam bed/seat for my little Morris Minor car 'Mavis', so that Dexter could be comfortable and safe travelling to local places of interest. The ramp on the other car was getting to be a bit of struggle now, a little too steep for Dexter to easily manage. Mavis being low to the ground was very easy to step in and out of. This luxurious adaption of the entire back seat (complete with matching scatter cushions) enabled social stimulation and allowed Dexter to continue to see the sights, people and places he loved. We were able to journey to and from appropriate places, pleasurably, where limited exercise could continue and enrich his quality of life.

At work, I was described as "a steel fist in a silk glove" which was actually a well received compliment from a respected and accomplished senior manager. Where animals are concerned especially, I am a softie, but in the right sense, of course. Animals need and deserve to be treated ethically and humanely. It is their purity of spirit, selflessness, love and loyalty that I am in awe of. We should all treat them with respect, compassion and love, as we would like to be treated ourselves. It was of utmost importance to me that Dexter lived out his days in complete comfort. Our pets deserve and appreciate what we do for them, all our love, understanding and respect. Animals are so accepting and never fail us as friends, family and the people we love can sometimes disappoint us in some way. To be very honest, I love all animals and I do not have much time for people with condescending attitudes who say that they "hate animals" and see them as less evolved or less intelligent. Animals are amazing, our equals and I feel they should be treated with respect. If we could all commit a little time to serving the animals that serve us then the world would be a much better place.

On countless occasions I was accosted because Dexter was out walking wearing a fleece jumper or a coat. I actually found myself explaining over and over again that he had a medical condition and this was the reason for wearing it. One day after receiving a barrage of abuse, I decided I would no longer give such rude people the time of day. Someone had actually wound down a car window and shouted at me for dressing my dog up! I was brought up to believe that dogs were given a fur coat to keep them warm. Neither Richard nor I had known a dog to wear a coat or jumper. Clearly Dexter's attire was not for fashion - those who know me will laugh and validate that!

It is so sad that some people can be so very narrow-minded. I once read a quote that said something along the lines of "dogs have many friends because they wag their tails and not their tongues". How very true indeed. I do wonder what the people would have thought if they knew that Dexter actually had his own washing machine to wash all his jumpers and coats. It was an old one belonging to my sister that she had passed on as it only worked on one cycle. Nevertheless, we were very grateful as Dexter's short, white Dalmatian hairs which, incidentally, have a little hook and are troublesome to remove from clothing (especially socks) weren't a great mix with Richard's Blue Fire Service Uniform.

Dexter began to drag his feet because his joints had fused, and his nerves were also starting to be affected. So, to prevent his nails from damage and bleeding as they had worn down as a result of this, he wore little lightweight disposable boots when walking on hard ground so that his balance was not affected and he could feel the ground beneath him. We tried many different types of boots before these, even ones made in Ireland specifically for him before investing in numerous repeat orders for the disposable ones which although did not last, suited him and his balance best.

Despite our best efforts, we again had a person asking if I couldn't get another colour of boots more fitting for a male dog?! They were purple by the way but really my only concern was for our beautiful boy's feet and that he was happy, if it helped and stopped the nails from bleeding. We walked on flat soft ground (grass) when it was at all possible but if he needed to go out urgently we either had to go into the farmer's field out the back of our house or walk down the bridle path at the front, so that Dexter could do what he needed to, where he needed to. He really was so clean that he did not like to toilet in the garden. Dexter still liked to walk into the village occasionally too, which meant pavements and wearing boots. Boots were made for walking and he wore them well!

Dexter really was determined not to let his health problems get the better of him. He was so brave, courageous 'where the mind is willing' really did ring true. We stopped going upstairs as the consequences coming down could be catastrophic for Dexter. Although he had a harness and a flexi lead to prevent jarring when he sometimes stumbled and lost his footing on a walk, we could not risk any stairs or steps. We all slept downstairs. I add here that I was more than willing to supervise and assist Dexter on my own, but Richard said that would not be right so we all stayed downstairs as a family. We loved and valued him, it was no inconvenience to us – we were totally committed to him.

Since we had to be very careful and restrict activity, we were extremely vigilant not to let Dexter engage in activities that could exacerbate some of his problems as a result of a slip, trip or fall. For example, he loved football but could no longer play and dive for the ball as he used to do. Instead we continued with the scaled-down version of the game and would carefully play pass with a small lightweight miniature football. Dexter would always return it with a tap of his foot with amazing precision. This little game, along with hide and seek that he had always enjoyed with his toys, could be played indoors or out in the garden. These activities stimulated his brain and senses.

He continued to take his baby football to swimming hydrotherapy sessions where he would glide across the water so elegantly to retrieve it. Swimming really helped Dexter. The warm water relaxed his body and increased circulation. It was brilliant as it is non weight bearing, kept Dexter fit, strong and he maintained his muscle strength and tone. Water therapy also improved his balance and co-ordination. I mentioned walking across flat soft ground but despite these measures, one day he caught his paw in a small hole in the grass and partially tore his cruciate ligament in his hind leg again. Another non-operative conservative management strategy had to be followed again as our vet had advised surgery was not an option. This method meant even further restrictions over a prolonged period of time. Some dogs are crated but such restriction would only further increase stiffness and limit flexibility for Dexter, so we continued as we were but with even more restriction and caution.

Poor Dexter, it was especially important to keep him in good shape and prevent him from gaining weight, so we had to be ever alert to his food intake. We were ever mindful "weight watchers" as although Dexter absolutely loved his food and it was one of his greatest pleasures, it would have been detrimental to his health to let him become overweight. Food had a huge impact on health and well being and a high quality, well-balanced diet ensured that protein helped wound healing and lean muscle was preserved. Everyday Dexter also enjoyed low calorie fish skin treats which provided extra vitamins and nutrients and removed tartar from his teeth. He very much appreciated home cooked treats that I would bake for him too. They must have smelt so good to Dexter as his nose was always up in the air like the bisto kid when they were cooking. I can't say that I relished the aroma of liver, oats and garlic myself but it was worth the effort as Dexter devoured them. Dalmatian's are notoriously VERY greedy dogs ... please take note, Labradors especially!

"Tuesday 13th July

Hair raising ride in Mavis today ...foot brake failed but fortunately the handbrake worked! With a paw of reassurance on my shoulder from Dexter, I was calm and didn't panic. Weirdest feeling coasting along towards the mini-roundabout... Thank heavens no-one was in front! We survived and managed to find a safe place to pull over. Rich was impressed when he came to recover us. Instead of worry, we had even made friends with a puppy (out on first walk). Dex was a perfect gent as always. Gentle and reassuring – such a good role model and happy to share his treats. Hope Mavis won't be too long getting 'fixed'. Me and Dex love our dog bus".

8

REAWAKENING

Many of us understand and appreciate that animals are often a source of solace and company. They help to comfort and cheer us in times of sorrow, upset or distress and help to lift our mood. They are wonderful, wordless, intelligent, sentient beings, each with their own unique personality. Animals have intelligence and an understanding that is beyond our words.

You may have gathered by now that I see animals as our equals. I love to be in the company of animals and I totally respect them. I wholeheartedly believe that we can communicate with them consciously and subconsciously too; we do not perhaps even realise that we are doing it. Some owners maintain that their pets understand every word that they say. Although sometimes, we are often saying something very different to what we think we are. You simply cannot fool animals. I could never fool Dexter where food was involved. For example one biscuit left in my pocket when I said that there were no more. Those with food savvy dogs especially, will know what I mean.

Many owners share an intense and magical bond with their pets. I wonder how many times you have heard people comment that their dog or cat was waiting for them at home. "They know, you know", owners often say when a pet shows empathy or concern when someone is poorly or getting ready to go on holiday (without a suitcase being in sight). These are very simple examples of an animal tuning in telepathically to their human's thoughts. Their animal knew when they were going to arrive. Dexter as I have mentioned before, always predicted when Richard, myself or even our postman was going to arrive (he did bring biscuits) but again, the same principle applies. Dexter was always very "in tune" and perceptive.

People have always commented over the years that I have "a way with animals". I do not know if you will believe what I tell you here, but I will share with you what I believe to be true. I am not expecting people to change their beliefs, it's for you to decide whether to accept or dismiss it. Many people are unfamiliar with the concept of inter-species communication (telepathy) let alone believe it is possible with our own companion animals; it was a revelation to me. I discovered animal communication because of Dexter; he enlightened me and changed my entire life. I realise that some won't entertain the idea or concept of this and I do not judge.

For us to believe, I generally feel that information has to be absorbed and understood, as opposed to just being accepted as a given. I don't know or need to know everything about how telepathy/animal communication works. I don't understand how electricity works and I don't question that. I do believe that animals are extremely intelligent and can pick up on our thoughts and words far quicker than we pick up on theirs. I am not a scientist or the type of person who needs to understand every minute detail. I can tell you however that animal communication is not some new fangled concept; even the legendary Barbara Woodhouse used telepathy in the wonderful work that she did with animals. Regardless of belief or scientific explanation, it is my hope that you come closer to the simple notion that animals are astonishing and characters in their own right.

It is my simple understanding that animals try to communicate with us in every way they can, but also communicate telepathically with one another too, meaning they can tune in to each other's thoughts. They are connected with each other and other species and are in tune at a deep energetic consciousness level. I feel that knowledge comes at the perfect time when you are ready to absorb it. I'd had a brief insight into animal communication but not firsthand experience. I decided to contact

Animal Communicator Jackie Weaver after buying one of her books, to ask her to communicate with Dexter to see how he felt and whether we could actually do anything else at all to assist him. I was astounded by the communication. Not only did she accurately describe Dexter's symptoms, she confirmed his personality and traits. Accepting of his condition, my beautiful and brave boy was most appreciative of everything we were doing to help him.

He had an opportunity to talk about himself but selflessly talked about me, how I was writing a book about him and how I could also communicate with animals too. This was a gift from Dexter for me taking care of him. He knew me better than I knew myself. I was completely taken aback. Yes, I was intuitive but could I really do this, and use this to help make a difference to other animals and their owners, I asked myself?

The session of animal communication with Dexter and Jackie confirmed a lot to me, including the depth of feeling and connection between Dexter and I. After Dexter communicated to Jackie that I could also do this, she most kindly assisted and volunteered her own animals for practice sessions. Although I was apprehensive and had no idea what to expect, I took a leap of faith and dived straight in to see what would happen. With Dexter patiently observing and encouraging me, I believed that this was possible and although I didn't really understand how, I opened my heart, cleared my head, gave it a go and let the communication flow.

Over distance, I communicated with Jackie's cat. Not really knowing what to do, respectfully I asked for help from him. He duly complied sending mental images, words, physical sensations and emotional feelings. What I accomplished in those moments I couldn't quite take in. I wondered did I make that up. Was I going mad? Nevertheless, I carried on regardless. I had nothing to lose. Surprisingly, the information (even the random stuff) was in fact correct. I was, and will always be so very grateful to be given this safe environment in which to explore. I couldn't quite understand how I was receiving this information, but it was a truly wondrous feeling to have this and the answers to questions validated by Jackie afterwards.

Jackie asked me further questions which only she knew the answers to (no-one could second-guess). I passed on the additional information I received. It was mystifying. We continued communications with Jackie's other animals. I was so very grateful and felt enormous excitement and respect to have communicated with them, yet felt both elated and bewildered too. I could barely believe what was happening, let alone discuss and share with family members and friends. I went for a stroll with Dexter in somewhat of a daze. Richard was out for the evening after being on an exercise with the Fire and Rescue Service all day, so I couldn't talk to him.

By the time he returned home I wondered if it had all been a dream.

However, my experiences, Dexter, Jackie and the animals that I communicated with, all helped me to totally accept interspecies communication as a reality. Which I now know myself to be true and deeply believe. Unequivocally it is real, and my experiences were certainly not a dream. I further tested my ability with pets who found their way to me and I visited Jackie's workshop when she started to run them. I desperately wanted to meet up in person with her and thank her personally, face to face. Jackie is very gifted, and I will always be eternally grateful for her help, support and kindness shown to both myself and Dexter.

I also attended courses run by the legendary American lady Amelia Kinkade, who is another awesome and very well respected Animal Communicator. Amelia has been endorsed by several academics across a number of scientific disciplines. She had the group engage in exercises that we would never have dreamt of and also explained the science behind the Quantum Hologram which I learned, put in very basic terms, is about the brain being a quantum computer tapping into memory using both quantum and space/time information. Amelia is so knowledgeable and passionate about helping animals and dedicates her life to a phenomenal amount of charity work. She is a beautiful person and wonderful role model. This is all so interesting and enlightening and her exercises and techniques have helped immeasurably.

For those who think this is all a bit farfetched, it may be helpful to know that Amelia has communicated with the Queen's and Prince Charles' horses. This is explained in one of her brilliant books "The Language of Miracles". Yes, you read that right, animal communication is used a lot more than one might think! Jackie has communicated with countless celebrities' pets (soap stars to Hollywood stars) and wrote a great book called "Celebrity Pet Talking" which really has helped to spread the word about animal communication.

People ask me if I have always been able to communicate with animals. To be very honest I cannot say that I remember doing so, although my family recall way back when I was approximately five or six years old, a little Joanne dragging a chair (to enable me to reach and open the lock and bolt on the front door) while everyone was asleep at night to let our family dog Laddie back into our house following one of his many adventures around the village. Not many dogs were neutered in those days! Laddie was a great dog and lived to the ripe old age of seventeen but he was very much a wanderer even in those very senior years. No-one ever heard him, or knew that he was back home until they saw Laddie settled in the kitchen upon getting up the next morning. I subsequently was said to have told my parents off, because after all, if I hadn't let him in then he would have been out all night long. I have always tried to put myself forward as a spokesperson for the animals in some way, shape or form.

Strangely, just after Richard and I were married, I dreamt that my sister's horse Norman, an Irish sports horse, was talking with me. I asked him "do you get bored out in the field Norman?" to which he replied "sometimes". I told my sister and family about my dream and we all had a good laugh about it. However, a couple of months later when Richard and I were house sitting at the place where Norman was stabled with two other horses (we were looking after all three and the two dogs) we got the shock of our lives when we couldn't find Norman in the paddock. He had jumped the river and was grazing blissfully on the lush grass in a nearby field ...obviously he did get bored "sometimes" after all.

My great love of animals helps people to gain a greater understanding of their pets through animal communication. This can be done over distance as well as in the presence of the animal, which means location need not be an issue. Normally I prefer to be given a photograph so that I can familiarise myself with the animal and make my introductions in the peace and quiet of my own home and I can concentrate without being distracted by the physical presence of the owner/animal. I realise that this might sound a bit bonkers to some and I hope not to be pulled apart or criticised if my explanation isn't thorough enough. Yet, if we can shut out distractions from our busy modern world and concentrate, it really is possible for us to learn to communicate with our beloved pets, our non-human loved ones. This can lead to huge breakthroughs and transformations. Animals have so much to tell us if we have the time and ability to listen.

Dexter made darn sure I was using this precious, innate gift. He wanted me to help animals and their guardians. He wanted me to be a guiding light to others, raising awareness of how amazing animals are and to share what I know to be true. I feel so blessed and grateful to be able to do this. It is a dream come true and it fills me with such delight. Animals, regardless of what some say, are not just "dumb animals". You will understand this for yourself on another level if you can communicate with animals. Patience, empathy, true love and trust are needed to telepathically connect with our pets. Interestingly, to explore this extra ordinary skill, we firstly need to reawaken our intuitive senses. I personally believe that we were born knowing how to communicate through energy like this, but may have forgotten how to do this consciously – although some of us still continue to do it subconsciously. Fear can block the process for some. Wisdom comes from sitting still and listening, being calm and opening your eyes and ears so that you can observe and absorb information and the complete picture; not from rushing to get ahead. Which, I certainly learnt for myself after many years of rushing around like a headless chicken. Work, work, work. I know all too well. I still live in the 'real world' believe you me. You too may be someone who has or has had a very busy life, constantly running around, looking after the family and so on.

It really is possible to still your conscious mind. I have my own process to get myself into a peaceful mindset that allows me to turn off noise, so that I can then connect and communicate with our beloved animals. I have conducted voluntary training for others with much success using this technique. It is hugely rewarding to see the utter elation when people experience connection and communicate with animals. Being an animal lover, having an open mind and a willingness to experiment is obviously a must to experience the wonderment and magic. I have had countless conversations with friends (on occasions, well into the early hours with a bottle of wine) about what this is like. I can only describe the mindset necessary for communication as quiet enough, able to tap into energy and a higher level of communication. I've heard it said many times that it's like tuning in an old TV or radio to find the right frequency or channel. Through a combination of senses, information is then revealed and explored by experiencing an animal's state of being as energy fields merge. I hope this simple explanation satisfies your intellect and helps to unravel any complexity.

With Dexter's encouragement, and after much effort,

came reassurance and wisdom. He and the animals I communicated with helped me to find my confidence and keep progressing. Through my experiences with animal communication, I found that it is simply best to tell the animal's guardian what I have felt, seen or sensed - basically, exactly what has been offered up during a reading. It is important to accept and pass on information and psychic impressions however nonsensical they may appear. It's not really my place to interpret the information, just by relaying it and then trusting the person to be able to clarify the information in their own way, information is deciphered and usually recognised – even if not apparent immediately.

I really had to trust my inner voice and intuition when learning about animal communication. In today's world this is not something many of us do automatically. We rely and are told to rely on, our logical brain. Richard was wonderfully supportive and accepting about everything, albeit it a little bemused himself at first. Admittedly, he had just returned from the pub when I excitedly announced that I had communicated with Jackie's dear cat Stanley 'Stan the man". Can you imagine! That initial look of astonishment was priceless, I think it helped that he was a bit tipsy to be very honest. He maintains that he never wants me to change who I am. I am fortunate that family and friends have embraced animal communication too.

To some who know us but do not actually realise

what animal communication is all about, I can only hope the explanation in this chapter will now serve to satisfy any curiosities. I would like to emphasise here that Dexter had made me aware of this gift to help genuine animal lovers and their pets, not to convince people of its existence. It is certainly not a 'parlour trick'. For a long time I was reluctant to even share the concept of this for fear of ridicule and sarcasm. Understandably, some people may be confused, as communication with animals can be outside of their normal experience. Mediums are acceptable to some, but talking with animals, 'really, yeah right' can often be the response. Telepathic communication is so very precious and I did not want scepticism to attempt to diminish the wonderment of this. Yet as I found my voice, people did accept, for the simple reason that their pets validated the reality. As I put my head above the parapet and have the courage to pass on the information gleaned, I am reminded that animals absolutely never, ever cease to amaze me. A great quote from A.A Milne, Winnie the Pooh ..."*Some people talk to animals. Not many listen though. That's the problem*". Makes one really think hey?

Dexter clearly had much to teach me. He partnered with us to help raise our consciousness and generously provided a helping hand. That he certainly did, by the bucket-load! We have grown because of him; he has enriched and shaped so many lives. Dexter enlightened and taught me to be a messenger for the animals.

Whoever would have thought that I would be writing this book about our lovely Dexter, and furthermore talking about inter-species communication in this chapter too? I still have to pinch myself! My Goodness, Dexter was so very special and I will always be indebted to him. I feel truly blessed to have Dexter as my animal soul mate, teacher and guide. I've heard all the jokes imaginable since I had the courage to speak out about animal communication, but the connection I have with Dexter has totally transformed my life and made me the person who I am proud and privileged to be. What he taught me has helped countless animals, their owners and animal charities too.

"Sunday 9th October

Poor Charlie Dog ...full of water and exhausted! River in flood and he decided to dive into the weir after seeing something that resembled a ball! Dad rang in panic, Charlie swept away. River was a torrent, totally wild. Dad just saw bubbles as Charlie disappeared underwater and under a tree that had fallen across the river. Rich, me and Sarah leapt into action. Rich ran one way following the river, Sarah, the other. I tried to remain calm and connect/communicate with Charlie. Unbelievably, I DID IT! Info was abrupt and precise – so strong it literally stopped me in my tracks! Clever lad. I was dumbstruck, couldn't believe my eyes when I instantaneously located him (it was going dark under the canopy of trees, he is black and Charlie was silent too, no barking). Miracle really! No-one could have guessed, it was illogical for him to be upstream, across the other side of the river from where he had dived in. Charlie, no doubt fuelled by adrenalin, had the fight of his life to get out of the raging water much further down and had somehow tracked along the thick undergrowth on the other side of the steep riverbank. Thank goodness he is a big, STRONG boy. How he managed that I don't know.

We were both overjoyed to spot each other. I kept calm and communicated that he must STAY where he was, until Richard rescued and recovered him. The look on Richard's face today proved to me that he now knows and totally understands just how <u>REAL</u> this is.

Trip to emergency vets confirmed just how lucky Charlie had been. Vet said we got him 'in the nick of time'. If he had dived in again to get back across or tried to track home by some other route he wouldn't have had the strength, and this would have been a very different story. Blimey, what Dexter has taught me has helped to save Charlie! Dex truly is an angel.

Charlie discharged with antibiotics (after bloods taken and given pain killing, steroid and antibiotic injections). He is so full of fluid and exhausted (too tired to eat). He can barely stand, let alone put one foot in front of the other. Vets want him back again tomorrow to monitor. For now Charlie needs complete rest at home to recover and lots of toilet breaks to hopefully get rid of the fluid. Hoping he is better VERY soon and no lasting effects. Poor soul, he's had us all so worried. Glass of port for shock! Mum and Dad so pleased/relieved to have him home.

Too late to prepare Sunday dinner - Takeaway tonight instead".

9

TIME IS PRECIOUS

I feel that my grieving process began earlier than the moment Dexter passed away. It was many months before when his condition was deteriorating further that we were forced to anticipate losing him. We despaired over the years that we had planned to share with him, which was especially pertinent as Dexter was a relatively young dog at six years old. We painstakingly researched, hoping to find new advancements and dreamed of a miracle that could take Dexter into old age. Sadly, neither Richard nor I could hold back time or perform a miracle. Deep down, we understood and accepted that we could not change destiny or stop the deterioration. Committing to daily regimes and making adjustments fundamentally improved our outlook, but we still felt unprepared for the intensity of hurting and heartbreak that was undoubtedly going to come our way.

We feared on occasions that the time had come but then to our delight Dexter would recover and be granted yet another reprieve. He was one of a kind and really had super-strong staying power. We had certainly got through some of the toughest physical and emotional challenges together. Richard and I had had to "man up" so to speak, be strong, rise to and live in the moment; but we knew that we were of course, very much living on borrowed time with our wonderful boy. Losing Dexter would of course be totally and utterly devastating and overwhelming, but we had to let go of our fears. Dexter was after all still very much enjoying life and showing us just how good life could be. He bravely soldiered on. He was so determined.

Sadly however, Dexter had a particularly challenging flare up of symptoms over what turned out to be his last Christmas period. We sought help and intervention and prayed for him to be given healing and support. His medications were adjusted (stronger conventional drug therapy) and his condition rapidly and thankfully stabilised once more. Mum was still in hospital at this time, having been there for several months. We worked with the physiotherapists and occupational therapists to organise her return home for Christmas dinner. There was much to organise, and we had to prove we were capable of assisting and providing care for her, but we did it and she did manage to come home for those few precious hours. The look on her face to be out of hospital was overwhelming and priceless. It was absolutely heartbreaking to see her have to go back to hospital when the ambulance taxi came to collect her but she did so appreciate being around those that she loved, with her home comforts, albeit for just a few hours. Quite how we struggled through Christmas, I shall never know. Dexter helped us all, as he always did and by golly he thoroughly appreciated his Christmas turkey. He so loved and appreciated his food and slept so peacefully and blissfully now that his medications were readjusted and controlling the pain and discomfort and he had a suitably full belly of course!

Combined with careful, restricted physical exercise and hydrotherapy to maintain muscle tone and mobility, we had found other ways to stimulate Dexter's brain and senses over the years which he appreciated and found fun too. He still enjoyed playing games of hide and seek with his toys and possessions in the downstairs rooms of our house, stairs were definitely still out of bounds as the consequences of coming down now, really could be disastrous.

Dexter especially loved nose work games. Another benefit was that it was quite tiring mentally and hunting out treats hidden in the garden brought him a reward. "He nose you know" we used to joke. Although, we fully understood why Dexter so easily located both the food and the non food items. He used telepathy, verbal clues as well as a combination of senses (especially happy sniffing) to take him straight to the relevant hidey hole.

Spring came and went and Dexter was doing really well. Come the start of the summer, Dexter was still able to get about unaided but sometimes unpredictably struggled to get up and out of bed or had difficulty rising from lying on the floor despite adjustments and modifications we had made to make his life as comfortable and as pleasurable as possible, such as carpeting over the top of our wooden floors in living areas and introducing large rugs in tiled areas.

Dignity was so important to our darling Dexter and we did everything we possibly could to ensure that this was maintained. We found that he was needing to go out to the toilet more frequently as time went on; he had started to develop stomach problems too, possibly side effects of all the medications. Our vet explored every avenue and prescribed what could help but we all knew deep down that he really could not go on forever.

Dexter's medications (conventional and homeopathic) were increased, changed or adjusted as frequently as necessary. His condition was constantly monitored with the aid of his daily diary. Fortunately our vet lived in close proximity and would kindly visit our home if Dexter wasn't doing quite so well. Otherwise, we would have regular appointments at the surgery. We routinely conversed on the telephone, every Thursday without fail.

Dexter progressively got more unsteady and on the odd occasion his balance was affected. His sturdy harness with a handle to provide support assisted and saved the day, but we had to face facts that his health was deteriorating at an alarming rate. We had to be so very careful to restrict activity to avoid the risk of a fall. One summer's day, Dexter collapsed in the field behind our home. I recall that he had twisted awkwardly trying to fend a fly from his back end and suddenly collapsed. I feared the worse but tried not to panic. Thank goodness Dexter had the harness on then as he was such a big dog and without that handle, and my sister and father's help, I do not know what I would have done. I called our vet whilst out in field and as instructed over the telephone, we carried him carefully to my sister's car which she had driven round to the field and it took the three of us almost an hour to assist him albeit steadily and cautiously into the house, resting and moving one leg for him at a time.

We settled Dexter in his bed and despite being in a great deal of pain, he still attempted to get up and reassure us all that he was going to be okay. He tapped and wagged his beautiful tail when my baby niece Jessica came into the house. He loved children so much, everyone in fact. Remarkably after only a brief period of rest, Dexter was back up on his feet again – that was how we was, so resilient and determined ...that episode was now over, gone and in the past. I was totally in awe and my sister and dad were flabbergasted.

It became devastatingly clear to see that now that Dexter's health was deteriorating further, that sadly there would be no more trips away in our camper. Dexter so loved to get away, we all did. Dexter was managing surprisingly well on the perfectly flat ground of his usual haunts, but the prospect of possibly longer walks and unfamiliar territory would be too risky. We treasured him and tried to keep him safe and protected. Our last trip had been to the seaside to one of his favourite beaches on Anglesey and he had absolutely loved it, but my heart was breaking seeing Dexter's quality of life potentially beginning to decline.

Reviewing his condition, medications and needs at this point and re-reading his daily diary entries confirmed his limitations. Despite all our love and nurturing and despite Dexter's determination and adrenalin fuelled joy for the sounds and sights of the powerful healing ocean, such long distance trips away were no longer going to be possible. Dexter's health problems simply would not vanish and such a big dog with spinal problems, mobility and travel needed to be carefully considered. We were ever observant and mindful, never wanting to let him suffer. Even realising the fact that we might soon actually have to make that decision (that dreaded decision that no-one ever even wants to consider, let alone make) was absolutely agonising. We made the most of the time we had and cancelled engagements that involved lengthy travel. We declined an invitation to Richard's cousin's wedding. It was a five-hour journey and sadly they divorced soon afterwards as it turned out.

Dexter courageously soldiered on and we made the most of each day and all those moonlit nights too when he needed to go outside. He always asked to go out and since we were downstairs with him, we were always on hand as required. I was able to take him outside in a timely manner which I appreciate was a big comfort to Dexter. It is remarkable how senses are acute and heightened in those small wee hours of quiet repose, when seemingly almost everyone and everything is still and sleeping, except for the rattle of an empty Large Goods Vehicle trailer, the call of a fox or a midnight train. Some of which sounded haunting.

I would stand outside with Dexter, waiting for goodness knows how long on occasions when he ate grass to make himself sick and feeling the retching myself. As soon as the vomiting was over, he would pick up his ball and with engaging eyes, attempt to ease my worry, by lifting my spirits and willing me to play. Dexter was wonderful, far braver that I could ever be. He was always so full of joy and fun. I don't know how he did it. The conventional medications clearly assisted with pain relief, but sadly since these had been increased, so were the side effects, evidently.

Spending day and night together, Dexter and I really were inseparable. We enjoyed spending precious time together, appreciating each and every moment, and the richness of love. Those ordinary, yet super special times in our world where he and I could just be. Comforting evenings, sitting snuggled up in front of the fire enjoying precious wordless moments, stroking those beautiful silky ears with Dexter's head rested on my lap. Or outside listening to the birds and enjoying the warmth of the beautiful sunshine and absorbing the sights and sounds of nature around us. On our little outings, with friends. All those simple, everyday fun times that we spent together were treasured. I dreaded having to even think about saying goodbye, to be very honest, I never wanted to spend a moment apart from my little angel.

I had bought a foam fold-up sofa type bed for my nieces and nephews to use when they stayed overnight at our home, but since Dexter wanted to spend more time outdoors when the weather was dry, I used this for him to lie and stretch out on outside. Dexter's need for comfort was paramount and we wanted him to be able to enjoy every precious moment that remained in complete comfort. Dexter loved the bed and I positioned it out in the sunshine wherever possible, repositioning and following the sun as necessary. Over the course of time he wanted to be outside more and more, on this bed watching the sights and absorbing the sounds. I would sometimes cover him up to keep him warm when the temperature dropped if there was no sunshine or there was a breeze, simply because when he was comfortable and warm he enjoyed resting blissfully and peacefully watching the world go by. He looked so happy and content lying there. People came to see him or acknowledged him as they walked past. Dexter loved the interaction.

I have heard people say that animals live in the moment and Dexter certainly did. He was an inspiration and truly heroic but we were constantly careful, ever vigilant and mindful to provide relief, care and support. We knew what he needed and when to provide the best possible quality of life. Dexter was comfortable and the medications and remedies were all doing their job controlling things brilliantly, but realistically Dexter would not be able to soldier on forever. We continued with short trips out in Dexter's luxuriously adapted little car to various destinations locally so that Dexter could exercise gently and safely and enjoy meeting the people and animals he liked to spend time with. As is the case with humans, I feel strongly that it's important for animals to enjoy social interaction even when exercise is restricted.

One day, travelling along in our little car to one of the local football fields (which is a well maintained perfectly flat area where Dexter could safely stretch his legs) I noticed a bungalow for sale. This, I thought could well be a solution to benefit us all, my parents included. It might have sounded a bit radical but if they were to move in with us, we could help poor Mum, who, now out of hospital was suffering with the physical and cognitive disabling effects of strokes and needed twenty four-hour care. Richard and I had been living downstairs for some time in our home enabling us to be on hand to assist Dexter at all times, so we weren't even using the upstairs of our home other than to wash and dress.

The bungalow would be great for both Dexter and Mum, as despite their courage and determination they really were experiencing difficulties; so, the bungalow could well be a fitting way forward for us all. Yes, it needed a lot of work. But it was also close enough for Richard to respond to call outs with the fire service and was close to my parents existing house in the same village, so was in the right location. There was a catch though - a big one. This bungalow was up for auction.

I discussed my hair-brained scheme with Richard and my parents (I'm not usually a risk taker) and we subsequently proceeded to make an appointment to view the bungalow. Dexter hobbled in over the back step when he came along and he surveyed each room enthusiastically like a seasoned valuer. His tail never stopped wagging especially when we looked around the old run down barn and walked out around the paddock at the rear of the property – it was perfect and Dexter loved it too.

Unbelievably, especially given the tight timescales, we managed to secure a remortgage offer on our house and clawed back some earlier overpayments made from all my days of work, work, and more work. So, we were ready and had a plan in place to guarantee the funds if successful at auction within the necessary time frame, enabling us to be able to pay the deposit required. With the support of mum and dad we prepared to go to auction – and what a scary prospect that was! A few days before the auction date I had a dream that Dad wheeled Mum into the auction room in her wheelchair and she put her functioning hand up. The effects of which could be clearly catastrophic especially if bidding was underway.

On the day of the auction, feeling apprehensive, I took Dexter for his routine check up at the veterinary hospital. On the way home we stopped at a nearby beauty spot and shared an ice-cream, I made him a mini cone out of the bottom bit of my cone. From the comfort of the car, we sat on Dexter's memory foam back seat, like two pensioners on an outing. We watched the ducks and swans on the lake and Dexter delighted in seeing all the children play. What would be our fate this evening I wondered; could we ever be a match for the big builders or property developers at auction?

We carried on, made our way home and later that night when Dexter was settled comfortably and peace-fully in his bed, Richard and I made our way to the auction room in a local hotel. We had arranged to meet my parents at the venue a little later so that we had time to reserve places. I said a little prayer that if this was meant to be, please help us to be successful at auction. I feel auctions are very stressful. Our home, savings, hopes and dreams at the mercy of an auctioneer. The bidding commenced but my parents still hadn't arrived. It takes a long time to assist someone with mobility problems, but I knew they would be coming; Mum did not want to miss this opportunity. Although Mum had communication and understanding difficulties because of Aphasia, she knew and understood exactly what was going on.

To be very honest what happened next is still a bit of a blur. Approximately five parties were interested and the bidding was well underway (getting near to our agreed maximum limit), when the double doors opened in the auction room. Dad wheeled mum in and she raised her hand to signal her arrival to us. At this moment, at the other end of the room, the hammer fell, but I had not even realised. I was still open mouthed seeing Mum because of my dream depicting this exact moment. I hadn't got a clue that Richard was the successful bidder or what the sale price was for that matter. Unbeknownst to me, poor Richard had nail marks on his hands where I had clutched so tightly. This was truly unbelievable, the synchronicity of everything. But we had only gone and done it, succeeded against the odds and under the guide price too ... unheard of! Goodness me, I could barely sign my name. I was shaking like a leaf.

We all went back to our house where Dexter greeted us enthusiastically as if anticipating our news and imminent celebration. When Mum and Dexter were comfortable and settled, I, in a bewildered state, poured us all a glass of wine. Wow, the bungalow really was going to be ours. I still could not believe it, and Mum, bless her heart, was so excited. Dexter looked so happy and content with those he loved surrounding him. He would be overjoyed to have Mum and Dad live with us permanently. We very much appreciated that time is precious and we certainly had some sorting out to do now, getting our house on the market, and fast.

"Friday 6th May

At last a short break away! Dexter was so excited to be back on very breezy Newborough Sands . Sad to see he's deteriorated since last time .Only a short walk. He lost his footing...the gusty wind scuppered his balance and he stumbled into a small pool. Unhurt, fleece jumper soaked but quickly changed (always a spare in the bag)! Resilient as ever and making his own determined way to the sea, Dex decided he was up for a run after playing pass with his mini football!! A treat convinced him otherwise. He absolutely amazes me, how he soldiers on, making the most of every single day and every opportunity. Safely back in our comfy camper, best cup of tea and cuddles with Dex, listening to the waves with the afternoon sunshine warming us through the window."

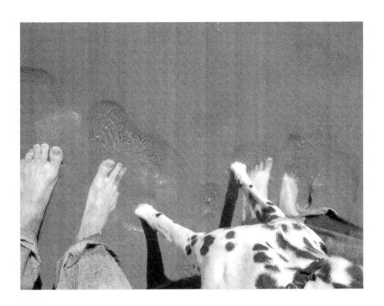

10

WHEN THE TIME COMES

Dexter was to be seven years old in the autumn and it was becoming very sadly apparent that it would be difficult for him to struggle on until then. He was valiant, determined not to let his health problems defeat him. However, a flair of symptoms had forced us to again readjust his medications, face our fears and discuss with our vet the options available.

After questioning everything, we decided all of us, Dexter included of course, that if the treatment plan did not control his pain, we would not prolong his agony. We had never seen him this ailing and infirm and it was absolutely heartbreaking to see him pace the floor until he collapsed with exhaustion. Dexter just did not know what to do with himself but after the additional steroid injection was administered, along with more pain relief and remedies he settled, and looked comfortable a short while later.

Everything combined looked to be controlling things. He slept comfortably and looked relaxed and free of pain and discomfort. We had discussed and agreed with our vet Mike that if the medications did not provide consistent relief over the next couple of days that we would be making that call that no-one ever wants to make and asking him to come to our home and help our lovely Dexter as only a vet can. Mike said he hoped that we would not be making that call to him and tried to reassure us that it might not come to that. This episode was the worst ever and with new additional symptoms too, especially related to Dexter's stomach. Not to renege a promise, we watched, monitored and waited fervently, and then fell asleep only to wake again to the same nightmare.

We had already spent a lot of time reading Dexter's body language and assessing what he was physically capable of doing. Now Dexter was deteriorating, critical decisions had to be made about what was best for him. Sadly, even his magnificent courage could not save him.

As devastating as this was and although I did not really want to face it, I had done some research already with regard to finding individual Pet Crematoria where we could take Dexter when that dreaded time came. I was fortunate to find a small, family run Pet Crematorium and Cemetery called "Sleepy Meadow" which was not too far away from our home. I feel it's important to do such research however upsetting it is, in advance if possible, to be assured of the service wanted.

Living in close proximity to the local veterinary centre, most upsettingly we had witnessed yellow bags being thrown into the back of a van labelled "Pet Crematorium" on a regular basis. Animals were hauled (I appreciate some would be heavy) from out of the freezer outside the practice into the back of the transit van with little regard or empathy, or so it appeared. It's very sad that deceased pets are left at some surgeries for goodness knows how long; many people do not realise this. Often, understandably, people are too upset to ask what happens, have not fully understood, or had the service they have been offered explained to them in any detail. Richard and I appreciate that everyone has their own views on this very sensitive subject, but we did not want Dexter's body to be handled in this manner after he had passed away.

Dexter and I had never spent a night apart and to think of his beautiful body being piled up in a freezer for goodness knows how long did not seem right at all. We felt that it really was far better for us to be in control, to give him and his body that had served him in this lifetime, the send off deserved.

I had of course also spoken in depth and in advance with our lovely vet to ask respectfully when Dexter's time came whether he could possibly assist him at home should we need to consider euthanasia. Travelling in the car and being put to sleep in the surgery was not what any of us wanted especially since travelling the considerable distance to the Animal Hospital Veterinary Centre would be difficult and uncomfortable for Dexter anyway.

Dexter was a huge part of our lives, he was our world and so important to us. We wanted him to be comfortable and treated with love and respect. Some people do not see this as important, but it mattered to us. Nevertheless, all things considered, I can honestly say this really was still the inevitable conversation I did not want to have. However traumatised we were, it was necessary at this time as it turned out.

The right intention is for the highest good of all and even when you know it's your beloved pet's time to go, not trying to save their life is very hard. We were emotionally drained and depleted but determined to make the most of whatever time we had left. Jackie, the Animal Communicator, confirmed Dexter's symptoms accurately and that us helping him was what he wanted. Of course I also knew and understood this, which is why I asked for validation. I still didn't want to face what was coming but it was comforting to have this extra reassurance from both Jackie and especially our trusted vet Mike that this was morally correct.

Living with Dexter was heaven on earth and it hurt unimaginably to think that we would soon have to say goodbye. The anguish was truly overwhelming, but we would not let or want him to suffer. Dexter's dignity and relieving him of pain was paramount. Later that summer's evening, Richard and I took Dexter for a very short ride in the car to the local arboretum that he loved. It was so peaceful and we made it about as far as the duck pond that was far enough. Dexter needed a rest before going back to the car and so we all watched the ducklings floating effortlessly on the calm, tranquil water in absolute silence. We had watched these little ones grow and now they were thriving.

What would we do without Dexter, how would we ever carry on. We would miss him so much. Eventually, we made our way back to the car and helped Dexter inside. Not one of us wanted to go home and face tomorrow but we had to.

Dexter's health problems however much we prayed for a miracle did not go away overnight, in fact the pain returned and became more intense as the hours passed. When he was awake during the small hours, he found it difficult to walk even with all the additional medication; every step looked excruciating. The pain from the conditions he was suffering from had now spread across his body like wildfire.

This pain was incessant and it was truly heartbreaking to see. Nothing was providing consistent relief, even when we administered further medications that our vet had provided should they be necessary. Dexter could not lie down comfortably, seemingly only when exhausted again because of the searing pain and heightened stomach problems that he was now experiencing. If I could have taken his pain I would have done.

Dexter wanted to spend time outdoors under the plum tree in the small hours. I stayed with him continuously as I had lovingly done so for so many nights. He was communicating and showing us, both Richard and I, that he had had his last few days, that it was his time for sure. Dexter was preparing for transformation and separation as this was an episode that was worsening. Clearly his conditions were no longer manageable; they were worsening despite all our efforts. As we had feared and promised, we now had no choice but to help end his agony.

We really could not let Dexter struggle any longer. Our special bond made it all the more difficult to do the hardest thing ever and make the arrangements with our vet for him to come and end Dexter's pain and help our beautiful boy continue on his journey. We made that choice as many animal lovers in such situations have to do for our beloved and devoted companions. This, we did out of love and especially as time was now so limited, we appreciated all of Dexter's love so much more.

Mike was coming later that day. It was Thursday and he was coming over to us at four o'clock. Tomorrow morning we were due to collect the keys to our new home; a home that we had hoped would make a big difference for both Dexter and my mum especially, with regards mobility. Mum and dad were planning on moving in with us since our new home was a bungalow. We had focused on solutions instead of problems to overcome challenges.

Both Richard and I had slept downstairs in our house for some nine months by now, to enable us to be on hand to assist Dexter when he needed to go out during the night. Stairs had become most troublesome for Dexter and so we had stopped going up a long time ago, as the effects of coming down would have been catastrophic. So, the irony that Dexter would now be climbing the stairway to heaven hit very hard indeed. We felt trepidation about our forthcoming move to the bungalow – it didn't interest Richard and me now, despite all our previous excitement and enthusiasm.

As heartbroken as I was, I managed to hold myself together, I remained strong and cherished this time with Dexter. He enjoyed a hearty breakfast of scrambled eggs at 5am served to him in one of my grandmother's beautiful china dishes as he rested in his bed. Dexter absolutely deserved the best. I could see that he was in some pain and discomfort, but he devoured the eggs, leaving only a few miniscule pieces. He took further medications and then settled at last for a brief rest.

It was such a beautiful day; it was as if the universe supported his impending passing. I went through the obvious as if to justify our situation. Dexter could eat and enjoy his food, but he now clearly was feeling an awful lot of pain and discomfort. He certainly could not walk as he could previously. Recently, he had started to have problems toileting. When he needed to go there was an urgency to do so and he was now experiencing trouble balancing to eliminate. He had always been such a clean dog and keeping his dignity was so important to him. Life was not going to be worth living, deteriorating at this rate, with such pain to endure and he did not want that. He must not suffer.

Dexter and I stayed outside on his foam bed for most of the morning enjoying the beautiful sunshine. I was able to assist him when he needed me. I recall a few days before we had a delivery and Dexter attempted to greet the driver. Dexter welcomed everyone to our home, he loved everyone so much. On this occasion, his legs would not hold him so I used the handle on his harness to steady him. Quite unexpectedly, he pooped on the drive before he got to the gate, something that he had never done before. Eliminating had taken him totally by surprise and this loss of bodily function we were told was the start of serious problems predominantly because of his spine and the compression of nerves.

Later that morning Dexter was quite chirpy but not so good on his feet, so I carefully assisted him into our little car and drove him round to see friends and family in the village to say his goodbyes. He trusted me implicitly and knew Richard and I would do right by him. Dexter was comfortable in his memory foam bed in the car that we had adapted for him and he was so pleased to see everyone. To look at him laying there it might have appeared to some that there was actually nothing wrong with him. He looked at ease and I could tell by non verbal and verbal clues that he was trying to raise our spirits. There was something about Dexter that resonated with all people and animals. Today, especially everyone loved seeing him and he would indeed be sadly missed by all.

Everyone we met and visited was so upset and very emotional, especially my mum, largely because of the emotional and behavioural changes that had occurred owing to her brain being affected following a series of strokes. We had always been a family where one kept a "stiff upper lip". So this emotion was really difficult and not helping me of course, but I had made my promise to Dexter to stay strong. I tried my best and somehow managed to do just that, with great dignity.

A friend of ours joined us along the way and we took Dexter to some common ground near one of the local children's parks so that he could stretch his legs. I had packed a little Tupperware tub full of chopped up sausages that I had cooked earlier to hand feed to him whilst out and about. Dad had purchased these for him from the local butchers shop as Dexter had always loved sausages as a very special treat. We had used sausages as a food reward during training when he was a youngster. He was so deserving.

Having done his business we sat in the park. Dogs are not usually allowed in the park but there were no children around and it felt appropriate to do so since Dexter needed a rest. We needed somewhere to sit a while until he could tell us that he was ready to return to the car which was parked a very short distance away. It was a lovely sunny day, beautiful in fact; the sun warmed our bones and tired bodies as we sat there.

We eventually and reluctantly made our way home. My friend left unable to speak, with a tear in her eye and Dexter and I waited outside for Richard to return home from work. I had a vase of beautiful yellow roses in the house, candles lit and soft classical music specifically for animals playing on the iPod to make our home environment as calm and peaceful as it possibly could be. Dexter had always enjoyed this soft gentle music. The yellow roses were symbolic, daft as it may sound to some, I very often sang "You Are My Sunshine" to Dexter. Yes I sang a lot of songs to him over the years and he seemed to enjoy this. I used to change the words to incorporate his name but this was my absolute favourite as he really was my sunshine. The sun was certainly shining today – the sun always shines on the righteous.

Dexter wanted to make the most of the sunshine today. We resumed our position outside on the foam bed enjoying some brief quiet time together, snuggled up

JOANNE JARVIS

until Dexter needed to move about again due to the returning pain. Yes we were making the right decision; I knew that deep down of course. I was strong and we could do this. But I really did not want to let him go. He really was my angel and my world. This was the worst day of my life, but we simply had to go ahead as planned, to be fair to Dexter. Sensing my anguish, Dexter took it upon himself to look and wait for Richard. He knew we didn't have much time left to spend together and he wanted precious time with Richard too before Mike came.

We waited at the end of the drive watching the world go by but I could not really take anything in. I supported Dexter with the handle of his harness as we stood there together side by side. We waited and sure enough very soon, Richard arrived. Dexter was delighted to see Richard return, he wagged his beautiful tail and gave his signature "woo, woo, woo" greeting that was reserved especially for us, his guardians, who loved and cherished him dearly. Richard looked rather surprised to see Dexter eagerly waiting; I guess the old saying that the candle burns brighter at the end rings true.

Dexter of course knew where he was going to be going. Although physically leaving us he would always be with us in spirit, watching over us and loving us unconditionally in all ways. We truly loved Dexter beyond measure yet continued to question ourselves over and over. Even now, at this late stage the answer was of course sadly yes. This critical decision was the morally right thing to do for Dexter. We always put him first and as hard as this was to accept, we had to be strong despite the agony and heartbreak and carry out this one last act of kindness so that Dexter could at last be free from pain and restriction. If not today, tomorrow or the day after we would only delay the inevitable.

The three of us sat together outside on Dexter's comfortable bed, the time passed so quickly. How I wished we had more time. Mike and his wife Jane (a veterinary nurse) arrived. To make matters even worse Dexter was as always pleased to greet his friend. Mike discussed what would happen and what we might expect. He was so caring and compassionate.

Dexter was calm and settled on his bed outside, this was how he wanted it to be. He was born outside and was to pass away out in nature too. I sat next to Dexter and fed him some more sausages, he was warm and I could feel his heart beating against my leg. He looked at me with such expression, the longing gaze of his soulful eyes conveyed how we all felt. Dexter was the most wonderfully brave dog. I reassured him silently. My silence being just another word for my pain. I stroked Dexter's beautiful silky ears whilst Mike painstakingly delivered the lethal injection and performed the euthanasia with great bravery and compassion.

Our beautiful boy slipped away and crossed over blissfully, quietly and so very quickly indeed. There was no struggle or fuss and to be very honest I was surprised just how quickly the transition of death came. Amazingly, I did keep my promise and somehow had continued to remain strong (on the outside at least) for Dexter. This had been morally the right thing to do. We all knew that and I truly hoped that Dexter's passing was as pain free as it possibly could be. I did not want Dexter to see me cry in his final moments. How I held it together I really don't know, but I promised I would and I did, for Dexter. I could do anything for him.

Such an awful numbness gripped me when Dexter's life ended and the reality hit me that he was gone. Richard was visibly heartbroken and Mike shed a tear too. Mike had known Dexter for a long time and he loved him, affectionately addressing him as "son" over the years that he treated and cared for him. Working as a vet is emotionally demanding and what Mike did took great courage. Having both Mike and Jane come to our home was such a comfort to us all and we very much appreciated this.

Dexter looked so peaceful lying stretched out on his bed in the glorious sunshine but all life was now gone from his majestic body. Whatever would we do without him – he'd filled our lives with joy and love. He was amazing in every sense of the word. He made life worth living and he made our house a home. A great sadness filled the air. I hoped this was a dreadful nightmare that I would wake from and all would be well, but that wasn't going to be the case was it. We all looked once again at Dexter's lifeless body, then Mike and Jane set off to make their way back home.

We had arranged to take Dexter to Sleepy Meadow Pet Crematorium ourselves. We had allowed for a couple of hours from the time Mike came out to give us some time to gather our thoughts, digest what had happened and give us time to travel there. Both Richard and I watched Dexter and willed him to wake but of course he didn't. We were going to have to pick ourselves up and remain strong for a little while longer yet, as we still had this final journey to make.

Looking up at the sky it was Richard who saw the shape of a face in the clouds. Doubled over with the grief that hit me, my eyes were now filled with tears. I began to sob and could not see. I know some people choose to brush off odd occurrences, seeing things like this as coincidences, but Richard was totally convinced that he saw the face of my lovely Aunty Margaret who had passed away some three years ago. Uncle Jack and Aunty Margaret were both massive animal lovers so this brought brief consolation that they might be looking down to comfort and reassure us. Dexter would always be well looked after, above all he was such an angel. Now he was with the angels.

"Thursday 26th May
Vets 2pm. Heartbreaking to see a German Shepherd in the waiting room in a very sorry state. Suffering terribly, in tremendous pain and completely off her legs. Unable to stand or walk even with harness/wheels. Mike sensed my terror having advised this could soon be reality for Dex."

....

"Thursday 25th August
Dexter finally resting/settled but I can't sleep. Randomly clicked on-line Guidance card with Dexter sleeping beside me. Gobsmacked (although I shouldn't be) to see the message..... 'Open the Door to the Kingdom of Heaven' is today really the day? Yes, I know deep down it is, yet still I need to ask as daybreak dawns as the last few days really have passed in a blur. There are 44 cards. This confirms what we already know. Our connection will <u>never</u> diminish but this is going to be so hard…"

FINAL JOURNEY

When the time came to leave and make our way to the Pet Crematorium, Richard and I looked disbelievingly at Dexter's magnificent yet lifeless body. Richard carried him to the car whilst I watched close-by feeling helpless and somewhat feeble. I had been so strong up until now, even though saying goodbye had hurt so much.

We had wrapped Dexter up in one of his luxurious chocolate brown fleece blankets. He had loved these, the colour almost identically matching his beautiful chocolate brown spots. We popped his favourite mini football (which he loved to take to his hydrotherapy swimming sessions) into the car with him, along with his soft toy Buddy, the big dog that he used to sleep with and cuddle up to. These items, including a single yellow rose were all put into the boot beside Dexter's bed in readiness for this, his final journey. He looked peaceful, at rest, yet we were bereft.

Remembering to lock the house in our dazed state, we got into the car and drove there in silence apart from the unpredictable bouts of sobbing. The journey didn't really take long but it felt like an eternity. Out of habit, I kept looking over my shoulder hoping to see Dexter's beautiful spotty face pop up from the rear of the car, it never appeared. On entering the gates we were apprehensive but maintained our composure. Susan and Terry, the owners of Sleepy Meadow were waiting for us as they had promised. They offered to help carry Dexter inside but Richard wanted to do this for Dexter himself out of respect. It broke my heart watching him struggle up the steps with our beautiful boy in his arms but somehow I once again kept a lid on my emotions. I followed him inside where Dexter was now resting on the table whilst Susan admired him. Both Richard and I were watching him willing him to wake up but of course he didn't stir.

We had opted for cremation rather than burial and were advised that because he was such a tall boy it would probably take about two hours or so. Susan read a poem which was "Rainbow Bridge". Richard and I sat on the little sofa stunned, now choking back our tears whilst we chose an urn for Dexter's ashes. Because we would soon be moving we felt that it was only right to take Dexter's ashes with us to our new home.

With this in mind, we chose a precious metal urn with two golden paw prints on the top. Even though this was one of the larger urns, it looked so small when compared to Dexter's body. After completing the necessary paperwork Richard and I left Susan and Terry to do their work. We were humbled to see how diligent they were, clearly honouring every soul that comes their way. Dexter's body would be treated with the utmost respect – he was in safe hands here.

While waiting for the cremation, we walked out of the pet cemetery gates and along the banks of the canal. We felt lost going for a walk without Dexter but we carried on, we had to do something. We stumbled along for I don't know how long, time didn't seem to matter a jot now. Finally, since it was starting to go dark we made our way back to Sleepy Meadow.

By the time we returned we could see the flames from the cremation incinerator chimney glowing against the night sky. We sat in the car to warm up not wanting to disturb Susan. Strangely, all of a sudden we heard singing. Rock music booming the same chorus over and over. The beat was so loud we could feel it in our chests. I recognized the words but could not believe what we were hearing. I wound down the car window to get a better appreciation and perspective.

Susan at this point emerged from the portacabin thinking that we were playing loud music from our car. She is a lovely lady with a unique personality and respectfully enquired "Do you like pop music?" We assured her that it wasn't us playing this but she could see that now for herself. This sounded like a live band. "How strange! I wonder where it is coming from" she kept repeating. The chorus continued over and over, louder and louder, we looked to the sky then at each other not knowing whether to laugh or cry.

The song was Kings of Leon "Sex is on Fire". I love this song and used to sing "Dexy's on Fire" whenever the tune was played! Dexter was so handsomely "hot" after all. The penny well and truly dropped for us now and my goodness... Dexter was actually, quite literally on fire. The music eventually stopped after Richard and I had both fully appreciated this rendition and taken in the meaning "Dexy's on Fire ... consoled with what's to transpire".

These words served as a stark reminder that I had of course made a promise to Dexter to write his story, the story of the life we shared and our journey into animal communication. Although his physical body had departed; I am and always will be consoled that Dexter and I are forever and eternally connected because of our love and what he taught me. The pivotal role he played in my life subsequently helps console others and of course raises awareness that communication with our animals is possible, even for so called 'normal' people, living regular, everyday lives, just like me.

We were utterly bewildered hearing the music as was

Susan. Lord only knows how this was happening, especially since Sleepy Meadow is in the middle of the Cheshire countryside making this even more pertinent. She had never heard anything like it in all the years she'd been there. You just couldn't make this up! We were in a somewhat remote location and there is only a canal nearby. The three of us wondered and discussed what the likelihood of someone singing that chorus live, over and over on a passing barge would be. Strange coincidence? We don't believe so. There was no talking, laughing or suchlike and to hear the same chorus repeatedly - the three of us certainly hadn't *all* imagined it. Susan verified again, over and over that she had heard and felt the music and what a strange occurrence this was. One might have questioned our sanity had she not heard it too. We had received and understood the message alright and when we explained to Susan so did she. In the darkness of the night Dexter was very much a shining light. Raising us up from despair and showing us that our love and memories will always be there.

Well, as if the music wasn't enough to contend with, when Dexter's ashes were finally ready (we had to wait longer than anticipated) there was another surprise. The urn chosen was not big enough to hold Dexter's ashes. I wondered whether Buddy, his ball and blanket had something to do with this, as they all went along with him for the final journey. Dexter had a magnificent physique but was ever so tall for a Dalmatian and he had the personality to match. Dexter was always going to be remembered for being larger than life. Susan was charming but clearly shocked as she explained that she had had Dobermans and Rottweilers fit this size. "Wasn't he a beautiful big boy" she kept saying. She began spooning the still warm ashes into the largest precious metal urn that she fortunately had in stock at the pet cemetery. I recall her saying "I don't want to spill a drop" as she requested our assistance holding the tray containing Dexter's ashes. It was a surreal experience but we chuckled about this, well what else could we do?

I guess tragedy and comedy are very similar depending really on how you look at it. Laughter is such good medicine and diffuses grief and tension. We settled the new bill which incorporated the additional cost of the new larger precious metal urn and made our way back home along the country lanes in the darkness. I was shaking despite Dexter's urn warming my lap. I always shake when I am emotional. What was life going to be like without Dexter? I dreaded to think about it. If ever there was a soul mate in animal form, Dexter was it.

We stopped to pick up some food to eat on the way home, in a nearby town. We realised that neither of us had eaten much at all that day. It was tasteless, unwholesome food but we needed something to provide some sustenance. When we returned home from the cemetery we discovered that Dad had thoughtfully left a bottle of wine on the doorstep for us. Richard picked it up and brought it in as I carried Dexter's urn in through the door of our now lifeless, seemingly empty home. It was raining and with the rain came floods of tears as the wine flowed. I have never cried or sobbed so much in my life, Richard neither.

Despite our exhaustion we didn't want to go upstairs to bed. We attempted to rest downstairs as we had done so for such a long time assisting Dexter. To be very honest, I hadn't the energy or the enthusiasm to climb the stairs anyway. We dropped off eventually but I still didn't really sleep. Sleep had become something that I dreamed of as I had been so used to listening out and caring for Dexter and because of my pain too. I didn't care for sleep now.

When daylight came it was still raining and the tears started flowing again. As animal lovers we get so much love and delight from our beloved pets and many of us grieve deeply when they die. I certainly had never seen Richard so upset and him I. Richard's alerter sounded dramatically breaking the silence in our home and off he responded on autopilot to an emergency Fire and Rescue Service call. I was alone in the house and plunged into a deep state of loneliness and despair. Today was a day which we all should have been looking forward to. This was the day we were due to receive the keys to our new bungalow. I realised that animals sometimes move on in order for us to let go and to move forward with our lives. Dexter's timing could not have been more pertinent, his departing was such a catalyst for change.

My life had changed in an instant without Dexter's special loving physical presence beside me, I missed being close to his beautiful, physical self. We were always together; Dexter was my devoted companion, my best friend. We had got through some of the toughest physical and emotional challenges together and he had truly opened my heart and awakened my soul with his special presence, devotion, wisdom and pure abundant love.

When Richard returned we went outside together and discovered that our front lawn was littered with tiny white feathers. Another message from Dexter, he was singing with the angels now.

Navigating through the epic grief that had hit us, Richard and I went over to our new bungalow in our bewildered state. We knew it needed a lot of work, but we were not anticipating or expecting Richard to literally fall through the floor upon entering for the first time! We didn't know whether to laugh or cry again but managed to chuckle. In the grand scheme of things falling through the floor really was of little significance. The weather was still atrocious, it was pouring. At least the bungalow didn't leak! It was dry, albeit bursting at the seams with woodworm. I had bought Dexter's urn with us. We didn't want to scatter his ashes at the home we shared with him and we were not ready to do this right away anyway. By chance, I discovered that the precious metal urn warmed up in the sunshine after I popped his ashes on the windowsill. Dexter always loved the sunshine so this brought some comfort in a strange sort of way. He will always be my sunshine.

When the rain cleared, family came to visit bringing food, drink, gifts and lots of children in tow. My brother and sister-in-law foster children in addition to having three children of their own. It was nice to hear the sound of laughter as all the children ran around the garden picking apples and playing games. My baby niece Jessica (my sister's daughter) took her first bite of an apple picked from one of the trees. She didn't know what to make of this at first, but obviously liked it as she wanted a second bite, grabbing my sister's arm and pulling the apple enthusiastically towards her. My sister gave us a slate sign engraved with the name of our bungalow. The sign was perfect and had paw prints engraved beneath the name, it was obvious to see that she felt awkward passing this on, but we thought it was really lovely.

When Dexter passed away my brother initially told his little ones the sad news, simply announcing in his own inadvertent way that Dexter had died. The children were devastated so I subsequently explained to them that dying (as sad as this is) is part of natural life and that Dexter's spirit had now gone to live in heaven with the angels. Many people believe that the spirit, or the soul of a person or animal lives on. I further explained that although we could not see Dexter's spirit, it is comforting to have faith that it lives on. I commented that Dexter no longer needed his physical body because when he died it had stopped working. He could not feel pain anymore now that he had gone to spirit. Dexter would be enjoying sleeping on a cloud in his spirit body in heaven and having such fun playing football with the angels and our relatives and other pets up there too – football was something he had loved but could no longer play. The kids accepted all of this, totally understood and were now smiling despite feeling sad and missing Dexter. These discussions helped immeasurably when my dear mum subsequently passed away too.

Ellie, my brother's youngest daughter and Paris who was a foster child of the same age (staying at this sad and emotional time with the family) made me a beautiful beaded bracelet. So much love and thought went into it and the beautiful rainbow coloured beads consoled me and reminded me that Dexter was over the rainbow never far away. I wore that bracelet until the elasticated cord withered. For sentimental reasons, I saved the plastic beads that had dropped off to serve as a reminder of this and something that Ellie said to me that day. Such soothing words of wisdom which I shall never forget.

At only six years old, Ellie was swinging her legs,

perched on an old bar stool (left behind in the bungalow by the previous owner) and confidently assured me that Dexter would always be with me and in my heart. How remarkable that a child her age understood, appreciated and was able to convey this. I gave the children some photos. Snaps of them taken with Dexter over the years to have as keepsakes – Dexter was such a gentle soul, a true gentleman, a gentle giant. He appeared enormous, towering over them in the photos. Dexter loved every-one, animal or human, and we all loved and missed him terribly.

I've heard it said many times before and this was highlighted on an episode of All Creatures Great and Small (repeated on TV) the opinion that some people actually believe that animals have no soul. The old lady featured in this particular episode who knew it was her time but was reluctant to pass over, was so worried simply because she was unsure whether her beloved animals would be in heaven. She had heard people (reli-gious too) say that animals have no soul, but James Herriot the trusted and highly respected vet put her straight and told her that her companion animals would be duly waiting to greet her - she then passed away immediately and peacefully. Animals are amazing souls, they are compassionate, loyal and loving and I believe that they deserve their place in heaven for sure. They are thoroughly deserving of all our love and respect.

Some people do not know how to cope or talk about

death for fear of upset. I feel that saying someone has "died" is very final and most upsetting for children especially. No-one ever explained that Laddie our family dog went to the vets to be helped on his journey to heaven. As children, we so wished that he would be made better, which he was of course, but not quite how we hoped. Mum wanted to spare us the upset and tried to shoulder all the grief and responsibility herself.

I was comforted to read that the word euthanasia was first used in medical context by Francis Bacon in the 17th century to refer to an easy, painless, happy death. If only Mum had looked at it this way and let go of any illusions of pain and suffering. She had absolutely done the right thing and she made that choice out of love. Euthanasia was performed in order to relieve suffering for Laddie, one last act of kindness; as was the case with Dexter too. Dexter although not an old dog like Laddie, had been so brave and had soldiered on for as long as he possibly could. To say he was amazing really is an understatement.

Dexter brought wisdom, goodness, love and joy to all. Time will not lessen our connection or Dexter's presence in my life. As a family we all believe and understand now that the ones who love us never really leave us. A beautiful soul is never forgotten. Our connection with them remains and they will be part of us forevermore. True faith is wholeheartedly believing in something that we cannot see or measure. Dexter taught us that, particularly with animal communication in mind.

The Rainbow Bridge

By the edge of a wood, at the foot of a hill,
Is a lush green meadow, where time stands still.
Where the friends of man and woman do run,
When their time on earth is done.
For here, between this world and the next,
Is a place where beloved creatures find rest.
On this golden land, they wait and play,
Till, the Rainbow Bridge, they cross one day.
No more do they suffer, in pain or sadness,
For here they are whole, their lives filled with
      gladness.
Their limbs are restored, their health renewed,
Their bodies have healed, with strength imbued.
They romp through the grass, without even a
      care,
Until the day they stop and stare.
All ears prick forward, eyes sharp and alert,
Then all of a sudden, one breaks from the pack.
For just at that instant their eyes have met;
As they see each other ...both person ...and pet
So they run to each other, these friends from
      long past,

The time of their parting is over at last.
The sadness they felt while they were apart,
Has turned into joy, for both in each heart.
They embrace with a love that will last forever,
And then, side by side, they cross together

— AUTHOR UNKNOWN

PASTURES NEW

News had spread of Dexter's passing; he clearly touched a lot of hearts. We were surprised but comforted to be inundated with cards and gifts. Dexter shared so much love, and in a way, it felt good that he meant a lot to so many people. This heartfelt sympathy was very much appreciated and really warmed our hearts. People understood that we were devastated to lose him and the offerings and floral tributes bought overwhelming sentiments of support but were no substitute for Dexter. We were grieving and broken hearted, yet we still got on with life as everyone has to.

We had a house to sell, so this forced us to move Dexter's possessions right away, ready for the photographer to come and take pictures of our home. It was so hard packing everything away – his toys, blankets, coats, jumpers, beds and bowls etc there was something of

Dexter's everywhere and his Dalmatian hairs appeared everywhere too. Despite Dexter religiously having the benefit of a daily brush, these coarse, white and hooked at the end hairs, had still managed to cling tenaciously to clothing, furnishings and all of his attire. I didn't want to remove or vacuum them away to be very truthful, but we were moving house. Having been inspired and exceptionally well trained by my obsessively house proud Mum, taking pride in our beautifully clean and tidy home, I really had no choice but to reluctantly enlist the help of the Dyson. We parcelled items for the dog's home and other charities but kept some of his treasured things, complete with his beautiful dog hairs.

We re-housed the kitchen unit that we had taken out to accommodate Dexter's bed. The house looked and felt very different without our darling boy's physical presence. It didn't feel like the warmest, most welcoming home it had been. Everyone who visited was visibly upset. Dealing with some inappropriate condolences and having to comfort and console others because it had brought back memories of their beloved pets passing (when we ourselves were grieving) was extremely hard but of course we coped. Some people just did not know what to say – there is clearly no offence intended, but it is terrible really that many people enquire "When will you get a replacement?" Can you imagine saying that to a person who has just lost a dearly loved partner, companion or child?!

Animals are unique personalities and have many of the same emotional qualities, just like us. We could never "replace" Dexter! Seriously, I understand that grief and mourning can be such a burden. However, this can be eased if we try to honour the love more than the loss (if this is at all possible after a passing). Sometimes, great changes really can come after a time of great sorrow.

We missed Dexter so much and even though we understood fully that it was his time to go physically and his presence was with us, we wished that he could still be here in the flesh with us. Sadly, he was not meant to be with us until old age and we had to come to terms with that. I found solace that my angel came to us in the form of our pet, even if, heartbreakingly, he only stayed for a short while and then departed as I seemingly found my purpose at this time.

One day, whilst looking through photographs of Dexter we were packing away, we were astonished to see something quite spectacular. Dexter was beautifully and uniquely marked with his stunning chocolate spots that we fully appreciated. But, we hadn't realised just how much this was so.

On the left side of his neck in a number of photographs we could actually see what looked like two angels connected in such beautiful form – this was remarkable and totally blew me away. How had we not noticed this whilst he was here, living with us? Perhaps because his markings would change shape as he moved around and we saw different shapes depending upon the angle we were admiring him? People often commented on how elegant Dexter was and how stunning his markings were. Richard and a very creative friend made a beautiful stained glass interpretation of Dexter's markings for me, which I treasure.

A group of young children living locally affectionately had nicknamed Dexter 'Chocolate Button' for obvious reasons. No wonder he was popular. What child does not like chocolate, hey? So many kids over the years tried to count his spots whilst Dexter would wait patiently lapping up all the attention and affection. I have to say we didn't actually try to count the spots ourselves so I don't know the number. Lots of people were attracted to his dashing good looks and Dexter's distinctive coat was so lovely to touch, being short and super-silky.

I'm glad that we hadn't noticed the angels before he passed away. This way, the angel markings felt like another gift that he'd bestowed. Appropriately so to be very honest, since I always called Dexter 'my little angel' and ultimately, because of our special bond we are always connected.

We were keeping our dearly loved Dexter's ashes especially safe with our imminent move in mind. Some people scatter their beloved pet's ashes in a special or meaningful place to commemorate the life of one so loved. We had thought of doing this with Dexter's ashes but then wondered whether taking a little of him to scatter in familiar and new places would help us to acknowledge our past and also our present.

We scattered a tiny amount where we were soon to move at the bungalow and a little further afield too. The majority of Dexter's ashes remain contained in his precious metal urn for now. This rests on my bedside and although this may not seem logical to some, will resonate with others. Even now, when I can't sleep at night, I put my aching, throbbing wrists on Dexter's ashes urn. It comforts and eases the burning pain. Someday, perhaps we will release the remainder of his ashes, if it feels appropriate and the time is right. However, should I depart this world any time soon; I have respectfully requested that Dexter's ashes come along with me.

Our wedding anniversary followed and then my birthday soon after. Opening cards without my personal wagg-o-meter assisting was no fun whatsoever but one tries to put a brave face on for the sake of everyone else. We were sad and we felt bad but we concentrated our efforts on clearing out the new bungalow we hoped to be moving into soon. Stripping out the carpets and furnishings left behind and so forth came as a welcome distraction. Our new home was clearly going to need so much more work than we anticipated.

After the rotten floor boards incident, where Richard had fallen through, quite literally, Charlie, Mum and Dad's dog continued to leap across the threshold when entering the bungalow, even though it had now been patched and made safe. He doubted the stability of the whole floor and he was in fact quite right to do so. Woodworm had done so much damage that the whole lot would need to be replaced. It was not strictly speaking too dangerous as we were ground floor level after all, but Charlie was taking no chances hugging the walls as closely as he could walking through the property.

We found it very difficult to be at our old house, the home we were selling and shared with Dexter, it just wasn't home now without him. Home meant serenity, cosiness and happiness and sadly it just didn't feel like that now. Maybe more so because we were moving. Since we had many prospective buyers viewing the house, we brought our camper to the bungalow and slept in there. This made things really easy for the estate agent and for us too. The house remained pristine, neat and tidy without constant effort. This worked a treat and unbelievably we received offers straight away. Thank goodness as buying the bungalow was a huge risk and as a rule we are not gamblers (especially me)! We would have had to rent out the old house should a buyer not have come forward immediately.

Much of our belongings went into storage which included Dexter's big memory foam beds. We could not store them in the barn or the bungalow because of the woodworm and damp. We gave away a lot of items, even our own bed; it would be a long time before we needed it and it was not going to be cost effective to store. A friend of a friend made good use of it.

The prospective buyers loved our old house but did not want a fish pond in the rear garden. When we were sure that the legal stuff was underway we set about moving the fish to our new home. Some people might have thought that we were crazy catching and transporting over 30 fish (with the help of friends and family) but goodness what would have happened to the fish if we hadn't moved them?

The pond, as it happens, was subsequently filled in when the house sale went through. The fish were hardy and survived the journey in a tank in the back of a trailer. We got some funny looks with water sloshing out along the road en route. They settled nicely in their new abode which pleased us. Dexter used to love to sunbathe on the decking at the old house next to the pond, peeping over mesmerized watching the fish. He would approve of us making the effort to take them despite having a million other priorities at this time.

The gardens, fields and barn and the bungalow all needed desperate attention and these things take a lot of time and planning.

The weather was fine and the children loved to come over and play outside. I set up obstacle races for the kids in the garden at our new place and my mum loved to observe these from the comfort of a garden chair. The children had so much fun, we all did, but on the inside we were still grieving.

Richard and I started to make plans about what animals we would keep on the land which needed a home. Despite this being our dream and ultimate goal, as much as it pained us, we had to be realistic and looked to renovate the actual living space first. This was especially important as dear Mum was deteriorating health-wise and we wanted to get things sorted for her as a priority.

We had always dreamed of owning land and felt blessed to have secured this wonderful opportunity. We had wanted a field of our own, a private area where we could walk Dexter safely, without worry. I still carry his whistle in my coat pocket these days. Symbolically it represents him walking the land with me.

Richard and I were inundated with people offering dogs to us as more and more people became aware that Dexter was no longer with us. The pleading and sad stories were very hard to deny but we were moving and were going to be living in our camper on site whilst the necessary major renovation and extension works to the bungalow were carried out. To take an animal at this time would simply not be fair. I was also spending time, as much as was possible, with mum (over at mum and dad's house) and both Richard and I, regardless of circumstances did not feel ready. Our hearts were still broken.

We had an impromptu party at the old house, which

appeared crazy to many people, especially since all the furniture was tucked away in storage. It was something we felt that we needed to do and I am so glad looking back that we did this. Sometimes it is human nature that leads us to spend time going over the past and time worrying about the future. We might miss the now, that being the case. Mum loved seeing all the children play and the adults enjoying themselves with a drink or two. It didn't matter that people were seated on deck chairs and were eating food off paper plates. Everyone had a great time that evening. There was such a lovely atmosphere.

Heartbreakingly, the very next morning Mum had a massive seizure and yet another stroke. Poor Dad telephoned in a state of panic and I soon found myself in an ambulance beside him, whizzing through the county yet again under 'blue lights' at break-neck speed. The sirens pounding, thumping through my head and wondering was this all a terrible nightmare? Mum was jerking uncontrollably on the stretcher. She was unconscious and sweating profusely. Honestly, Mum was strong but how much suffering can someone take. This felt so unfair.

Our whole family was distraught whilst Mum was yet again assessed in hospital. Unable to communicate her wishes and feelings to those who were tending to her because of her aphasia she looked weak and positively helpless. This was not my mum. I was crying inside but wouldn't let anyone see. Mum didn't want a 'wimpy' daughter, she needed to get out of this environment and needed assistance and nurturing from those who loved her, in her own surroundings where she felt safe. We understood her and took the time to do so, even though it was hard.

Three days later, the day we actually moved house there was a hoar frost. The last of our possessions were bundled into boxes and the house was given a good hoover and the skirting boards given a final dust down on our way out. Mum was extremely house proud and had she have been capable would have been assisting in these cleaning tasks I am sure.

We had a good look around all the rooms before closing up for the last time. Spookily the fire alarm started to sound. Funny really, with Richard being a Fire fighter. Was this Dexter from another plane somehow engineering this to lighten the mood? We loved this old house and all the memories it has held, this will be so forever.

Nevertheless there was no time for sentimentalities. Mum was "no nonsense", and I had to go to the hospital and visit her. Dad and I were looking forward to giving Mum the long-awaited news that she could come home again tomorrow, all being well.

Richard and I drove in bittersweet silence to our new home. There were blue skies and although it was freezing cold weather, everywhere looked beautiful because of the frost. Our trees, our fences, the land was magical with crystalline deposit of frozen water vapour. We couldn't quite believe it or take in the fact that we had officially now moved home. Perhaps it would register after sleeping permanently, night after night, in our camper since the bungalow was not yet habitable. We would be absolutely fine in onesies and numerous quilts and sleeping bags, hey?

Nonetheless, we were reassured that this move was absolutely meant to be. "Rest in peace Dexter our most loving and gentle lad", I murmured, clutching his ashes. Thank you again for guiding us here and the wonderful time that we had. Our new postcode ended with the letters 'DE'. After putting a kiss 'X' at the end of the postal code on a text message to advise our new address …here was written confirmation, right before our very eyes that 'DEX' would always be with us at our new abode.

"Wednesday 16th September ..For <u>Dexter's</u> Diary
In memory of Dexter, back in the seat today doing
animal communications. Arghh I so miss him doesn't
feel the same doing this without him physically beside
me, but I only have to relax and close my eyes to feel
my special mentor's presence . Never heard of a cat
eating CRISPS before! Lovely Welsh 'cheeky' character
showed me piles of empty packets to really get her
message across. Had to laugh, it was all so true! This
one deserves a mention in the diary! I am so grateful
for this incredible innate ability and my connection
with Dex that is as strong as EVER."

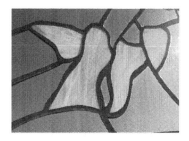

SOMEONE TO LOVE

Soon it was spring and glorious yellow daffodils bloomed. The front lawn was overflowing with different types and shades. I never knew that so many varieties of daffodil existed, nor had I seen so many in one place. They were gorgeous. The old lady and her daughter who lived at the bungalow previously had clearly taken great pride in tending to the garden. These lovely ladies had also looked after the visiting birds, something that we also continued to do.

Dexter very much remained in our thoughts and hearts. He would have loved living here, but he was meant for higher things. I dreamt about him a lot and received messages and insights from communications but I was lonely without his extra special physical presence beside me.

One night at the beginning of May, I had a dream, a

vivid dream about a predominantly white cat called 'Sophie' with orange and black markings. I had carried out some animal communications for two cats of the same name but this was neither.

The dream was so clear and the guidance I subsequently received so precise, that without question I immediately called the local Animal Rescue whom I had helped previously. Could this be Dexter's intervention? Through my dreams, was he sending me someone to love?

I enquired whether they had a cat currently in their care, named 'Sophie' and as described above. I was dumbfounded to be told that "yes" they did but we wouldn't want to take this one as she was feral, wild, a 'killer cat'!

We were still living in our camper at this time and just the other week a mouse had got in. I screeched in the middle of the night as I felt the curtain move, yet Richard tried to convince me that I had imagined this. He could sleep on a washing line that one, through any amount of noise whilst I am a light sleeper.

As it happens, I hadn't imagined a little creature running around at all. The next morning the evidence was there to see. There were mouse droppings (Yuk) on the unit and the 'imaginary' mouse had eaten approximately a quarter of a banana from the fruit bowl! We had to clean and sterilize everything. I couldn't tell Mum about this of course. She would be absolutely horrified to hear vermin were ransacking the place.

Now I had the solution to our rodent problem. I told the rescue I was coming to collect the little cat tomorrow. This was going to happen and would be a win win situation. The odds had been against this Calico cat being adopted up until now.

There was no discussion, no hesitation; this was absolutely the right thing to do. I told Richard all about the situation, that I was going to collect this little cat and could he kindly make the barn safe for her. She would need a safe space for a number of weeks at least until she became accustomed to her new environment. He wasn't too impressed, I have to say, he was up to his eyes doing works here and I was adding to the list of jobs. Nevertheless, he happily complied when I explained that this was the cat I'd dreamt about and I was saddened to hear that this little cat had been in rescue for two and a half years and desperately needed a home.

The rescue told me that she would never go in a house and wasn't at all friendly. She needed an outside space and we had a barn. Perfect. I borrowed a cat basket from my friend Sarah. Her stunning cat Poppy had found herself a five-star home via this rescue some time ago with my help. Sarah was only too happy to help.

My friend Lisa came along in her little car and offered a lift. We picked up the cat basket en route and continued the short distance to the cat rescue via the pet store. Lisa did not know at this time about the process of animal communication. I hadn't found the right moment to explain. Inevitably whenever the topic is discussed at length or comes up in conversation, people are curious and often have quite a lot of questions.

Whilst Lisa was chatting away in the car, I took a few deep breaths and quietly tuned into the energy of the little cat we were going to meet shortly. I respectfully put across that our intention was pure; we had no expectations of her, just for Richard and me to offer her a home and the freedom she deserved. If she liked me, I asked her to please show willingness as her sign, to confirm that she would like to come home with me today.

I would like to point out here that I had never had a cat before. Richard had, but not me. I would have loved to have had one as a child but my mum didn't particularly like cats, so this was not to be. I had very little practical experience and knowledge of the fabulous feline species, only that what I had learnt from the cats I had communicated with or helped to rehome. The "Cats Sleep Anywhere" and other poems book that I had as a child couldn't be taken into consideration as reference material.

Lisa and I collected everything a cat would need from the pet store and then arrived next at the Cat Rescue. John, the lovely gentleman who runs the rescue, was visibly shocked when 'Daisy' as she was now going to be called (with her blessing of course) came out of her small, elevated pen of isolation to greet me. She took a moment or two to sum me up and then daintily and quite remarkably climbed into my arms. I was mesmerised by her.

John explained no-one had been able to get really close to her, whether that be other cats or humans. Sophie was feral, fierce and so she was labelled 'a killer cat'. If people came to look and touched her, she would scratch them, perhaps because she was taken unawares and didn't actually want them to come close. She had given the carers 'love bites', so he called them. I think there were a few choice words in there too. I believe this was because she enjoyed a little contact and after a certain amount of time became frightened. She scratched or gave a 'love bite' at such a point. How else could she convey this?

Being confined in a small area and the power of the objectionable words describing her had a profound influence. This controlled rescue environment created a formative experience. For many years, prior to being captured with one of her many litters of kittens, when 'Sophie' was existing in a wild state and had to not only fend for herself but also protect her brood, she had to constantly keep her wits about her. This instinct clearly continued in this rescue space, she was at all times hyper vigilant.

When her babies that were raised by her in the rescue centre were considered old enough, they were 'taken' from her and found homes. Sophie was then transported to the vets. This was another completely alien and terrifying environment. The smells and sounds not to mention drugs/chemicals and surgery. Here she was neutered which was certainly the most sensible and considerate thing to do as there had been numerous litters of kittens beforehand. She didn't know what was happening to her. Sophie was then returned to the rescue centre where once again she was safe, albeit caged, trapped (in her view) until now. However, her luck was about to change.

How much had this incredible girl suffered to continue to put on this show of being wild and tough as old boots, I wondered? Her mind definitely had become that which was perceived. She played up to the role of the 'killer cat'. What else could she do? She hated the cats that John attempted to buddy her up with for company. John is a kind, knowledgeable man and tried to help her. He is incredibly dedicated, having been involved in animal rescue for 30 years. Although by his own admission, he didn't totally understand Daisy. John reiterated that she would never be suitable for a normal domestic home.

She needed her own space and lots of it. The cats he introduced were a threat to her, not company; she was frightened and didn't want them in her space. I guess it's comparable to us having to share our bedroom or even a prison cell with a stranger whom we don't like the look of, or perhaps don't trust. It was bad enough for Daisy having cats surrounding her, below and to the sides in separate pens. She reacted the only way she knew how.

Although she was very well cared for in rescue from our point of view, in the sense that she was given food and shelter and was safe from outside influences, this must have been a living hell for Daisy. Caged up for those years was incredibly hard. She had previously been a free spirit, able to roam the countryside and hunt, whenever she pleased.

How could she really trust humans when they had captured her, imprisoned her here and then taken her babies away? This was a peculiar environment. She was frightened but how could she show this or explain it? Fear is a sign of weakness in the animal kingdom.

Deep down I sensed that this little cat, who was now coming home with me, was full of love. Quite simply she felt vulnerable, albeit safe from harm, at the rescue centre. I respected and loved her from the moment we set eyes on each other. We had an instant connection, I understood her even though I didn't know much about cats and unbelievably she trusted me already. She had waited for the right home, even though she had to wait a very long time. This showed enormous patience and strength of character to me. I was in awe. Richard and I would give her the time and gentleness she needed in order to heal; Daisy would continue to be safe with us, off the streets and not have to worry about finding food and shelter.

Surprisingly, Daisy allowed me to stroke her (I asked her permission first) and then she climbed in the borrowed cat carrier herself. In my head I had shown her what would happen next (rather like a short video clip). To get to where we were going, her new home environment this was what she needed to do. I paid the adoption fee which was miniscule considering all the care and costs involved in neutering Daisy etc. I thanked John and promised to give him an update. She was as good as gold on the twenty-minute journey home, in the cat basket placed on my knee.

Richard was eagerly awaiting Daisy's arrival. Thank goodness I have a trusting husband; he hadn't even seen a photo yet, let alone met her at this point. He had got the back of the barn ready for her and had also proudly put up a sign 'Daisy's Den'. She was going to be so loved.

Daisy tentatively explored her new surroundings when we opened the cat carrier door and gave her access to her barn. This space must have felt enormous. Taking into account her background and given the fact that this was only her first day here, we were comforted to see that this tough little cookie had already started to come out of her shell.

In the barn, we had re-housed an old leather sofa which had been left behind in the bungalow by the previous owners. That first evening Daisy actually came to sit on my knee. I didn't ask her or encourage her to do this; she did this because she wanted to.

I was astounded and felt so privileged that she trusted and wanted to come so close to me. The reverberating purrs, that wonderful sound that emanated from Daisy's chest, something I had never personally experienced, felt or heard before served as confirmation that Daisy felt comfortable with us and proved she was indeed a friendly little 'Barn Cat' too.

We popped the cork on a bottle of Prosecco to celebrate Daisy's arrival and guess what …she absolutely LOVED playing with the cork. We were now positive that Dexter had a hand or rather a paw in this and would wholeheartedly approve. Furthermore, realising the significance, when we observed that her fabulous fur coat bestowed a beautiful orange paw print marking.

Daisy was a very special little girl. We were going to be helping her to embrace new experiences and move forward without fear. Daisy was already helping us to enjoy life again. It just goes to show that when your heart has been broken with grief, pain or fear, what follows can be a time when it opens once again to more love, if you are receptive. Turning the tragedy of losing Dexter into something purposeful had made me realise that loneliness was not the same as being alone. The loss and impact on my heart and soul was for sure both a physical and emotional wrench. There were always plenty of people to do something with, but I missed the special animal presence close to me, to do nothing with. We felt honoured Daisy had waited for us to give her a home and ultimately her freedom once again. She was so deserving.

In contrast to Dexter's arrival Daisy barely ate a morsel. Having had a lot of kittens previously, she has a saggy belly which wobbles when she walks. This is how she is, a reminder of who she is, and it makes her even more gorgeous. Some 'big girls are beautiful' as the song goes and in Daisy's case this is not because of over eating, she eats like a sparrow.

People can be quite rude insinuating that Daisy is obviously 'well fed'. They don't know her and what business of theirs is this anyway? Even though the vets said that her primordial pouch is predominantly on account of having so many litters of kittens, some people seem to 'know best' and enjoy voicing their opinion. Can you imagine going up to someone and saying for example, 'your daughter's well fed, isn't she?' The backlash would be immense. The same would apply if one was rude to a lady who had numerous children. I am sure you can comprehend what I am saying. Both people and animals can have different metabolisms. Everyone is unique regardless of species; we are all different shapes, sizes and have different personalities.

Incidentally, the food, (recommended by John) that I purchased from the pet food store was not enjoyed at all.

I gave the bag which was a high quality, reputable brand, I might add, to the rescue since this is what the cats there were fed. Daisy ate only a tiny amount of the new food (again high quality) which I gradually introduced her to. She preferred mice and there were plenty to catch in the barn. Daisy provided a valuable service mouse catching. I honestly do not wish to eradicate mice from the earth, but our barn had become somewhat a 'mouse magnet' at the time. Daisy helped to protect and save our worldly possessions in store here. Many of the mice moved out voluntarily. Daisy helped maintain a balance in nature. John was thrilled to hear that Daisy was enjoying her new home and a natural life.

We observed that Daisy didn't taunt, torture or 'play' with mice as some cats do. She simply caught them, killed them and then ate them. She showed us what she had had to do to survive. Daisy was a skillful huntress and must have been the most wonderful mother to her kittens, steadfastly protecting and providing for them. Teaching them right from wrong with her 'no nonsense' direct approach would have helped them to make their way in the world.

The barn, although large, had a concrete floor and it occurred to me that Daisy had not stepped foot on soil or grass for all the years she was at the cat rescue. I asked Richard if it was at all possible to extend Daisy's quarters to include a south facing 'sun room' with just the rough ground at the back of the barn as the floor. Nothing fancy but yet more work. He wasn't too impressed at the suggestion but nevertheless made the alterations and a small area was made safe for Daisy to step out onto the grass when she wished to do so.

We had a couple of builders doing some bricklaying here at the time and one in particular was a cat lover. Richard and the two guys watched intently as Daisy stepped off the concrete and tentatively onto the grass. She could seriously not believe how good it felt, but by golly did she do a good job at showing us. When she started to roll over on the grass amongst the daisies, the bliss was evident. There was not a dry eye observing.

Daisies symbolise new beginnings and are a delightful sign that spring is here and summer is on the way. Daisy was obviously a fitting name.

Even though she would only have to use the barn and her sun room for a relatively short amount of time, this half way house was clearly most appreciated and provided a taste of the outside world that she had missed so very much.

Richard and I made a conscious effort to spend time with Daisy in the barn in the evenings. As soon as I came back from my parents' house, and Mum was settled, I found that I couldn't get home quick enough to sit with Daisy and enjoy her company. Despite her rough start in life, she was quickly settled and thriving. Daisy was starting to show her sweet and affectionate side and was fun to be with especially as we had bonded and started to play together.

Soon, the day arrived when we could open the gate and Daisy could wander from her barn without restriction. Richard, my friend Sarah and I were astonished that she followed us whilst we walked the perimeter of the fields. I felt it was important to show her where our property boundaries delineated. Not a dry eye, again.

Daisy had freedom now and yet she had chosen to stay with us. We felt honoured she actually wanted to be with us. When night-time came, Richard and I went to the camper to sleep as was the norm for us at this time. It wasn't long before we heard a 'Squeak' at the door. What on earth was it? Not another mouse? Richard opened the door and there was Daisy sitting on the step outside. She didn't scratch the door she 'squeaked' the door with the pads on the underside of her paw! We let her in of course and most nights she slept in there with us, unless she was on 'watch duty'.

Daisy is a most effective, competent 'manager' and thoroughly deserving of this title. We have on occasions actually seen this fierce protector chase off a fox, not to mention numerous amorous, territorial male cats. Some of them are not at all nice and the scent left behind is absolutely vile! Daisy chased off a person twice, someone who categorically 'hated' cats and whom we never saw again. One had to see this to believe it, I hasten to add.

Although a keen mouser, Daisy does not catch birds

as a pastime. In fact, Daisy has much love and respect for our feathered friends. Demonstrating ultimate compassion and a softer side, Daisy once gently picked up a fledgling robin that had failed on first flight. She carried it to Richard and released it into his outstretched hand. He was then able to pop in safely out of harm's way onto a perch, a joist on the lean-to at the back of the barn. When the stunned little bird had recovered it flew off, thankfully making a successful flight this time. The mother later landed and sat on Richard's head when he was working in the barn. Perhaps this was an obligatory 'thank you'? Regardless, this was quite a sight.

Daisy, such a clever cat, learnt left and right paw instantly. Yes felines really are responsive and enjoy training like other pets. She came to her name when called, could climb ladders and climb back down again too. This was very handy because of all the works going on. It would have been very embarrassing if I'd had to call the fire brigade.

Even in the early stage, I never had to telephone and notify Richard that I was on my way home. Telepathically in tune, dear Daisy would be waiting on our drive. Always five minutes prior to my arrival, whether that be on foot or by car, Richard commented that Daisy would seemingly just 'pop up' out of nowhere.

With time and complete sincerity and commitment, Daisy has learnt that she can fully trust us. She has overcome many fears, anxieties and inhibitions and is a super character. We comfort and respect each other. Daisy has made me wiser and enlightened us all in the ways of the fabulous feline species. Even people working in animal professions. Daisy is the exception, rather than the rule, that a feral cat is now tame.

Nevertheless, the lack of exposure to humans and having never been taken to a veterinary surgery as a youngster has resulted in Daisy becoming stressed when taken out of her territory. We are most fortunate, however, to have an accommodating and knowledgeable veterinary practice. In particular, an exceptional, under-standing RVN Head Nurse, Jenny, who assists with Daisy's treatment with compassionate concern. She is fabulous and totally adores cats.

I feel that it is imperative that children have a high regard for animals. As stated in the famous lyrics "I believe that children are our future, teach them well and let them lead the way". Animals will then "show them all the beauty they possess inside". We really must guide children as best we can regarding how to behave around animals, since this will determine their future. Daisy has educated my animal loving nieces Jessica and Isla to the highest degree. This knowledge and under-standing has been eagerly absorbed and will subse-quently be imparted through generations I am sure. These clever little characters have already educated their elders. This is a joy to see and will ensure that any animal that shares their home or crosses their path will have all the love, attention and respect that they rightly deserve.

Signifying kinship, mutual loyalty, love and understanding, our little Daisy is a much-revered companion. What a lucky girl I feel to have such an amazing heaven-sent cat.

14

LEADING LIGHT

The bungalow was slowly taking shape. Ian, my brother-in-law, was busy installing the heating and water systems for us and Richard was assisting his brother. We had allocated a lovely large wet room for Mum, having converted one of the bedrooms. We had also made provisions so that the entire ground floor was the same level throughout; this was to provide safe, wheelchair friendly access. We hoped that this would make a big difference to her lifestyle and that Mum was going to love living with us at the bungalow. It had been hard watching her independence being eaten away by medical conditions.

I had been over to my parent's house already that morning but then had an alarming telephone call from my dad to please, return urgently as Mum had bumped her head. Having had several strokes, Mum had become partially paralysed, so it was very easy to fall, even from a seated position. She could no longer stand unaided or rise from a seat herself but she never gave up trying. Mum had toppled headlong and bumped her head on the radiator that was in close proximity. Dad was distraught as he was just a short distance away in the same room, but sadly could not feasibly catch her or break the fall in time.

I told Richard what had happened and together, we went straight outside to our car. A white feather floated down from the sky above, landing right in front of me as I walked. I recall feeling, once inside the car, that the drive was happening in slow motion during the course of this short journey. Neither Richard, nor I uttered a word.

We were most relieved to find that Mum was completely coherent and most surprisingly trying to crack a joke when we arrived. She had aphasia so things were difficult to understand sometimes, but we got the gist. She seemed brighter than she had done for some time. Richard and I further checked her understanding and carried out a visual inspection on her. Although she looked remarkable, we still wanted to get Mum checked over by someone working in the medical profession. We tried our best, as had Dad, to insist on her going to hospital to be medically examined or even a visit to the local Health Centre.

Mum was having none of this. She had spent too much time in such environments. She detested hospitals and who could blame her. We decided we would closely monitor her for a short while and then try once again to persuade her to go and get checked over. We had a bite to eat and a drink.

Richard was instructed to go home. Dad went out (also as instructed) to walk Charlie, their dog. Charlie was dad's lifeline and dad didn't dare object to mum's request. I stayed with Mum and performed the monotonous task of a little ironing under her watchful eye. I am not very good at ironing, I don't like it. I struggle with it because of pain and restriction, but Mum was always very particular about such things, so I always tried my best for her sake.

Mum was sitting in the chair next to the lounge window. She always liked to watch passersby from this spot and would wave to familiar faces with her good arm and hand. She couldn't really follow what was on the television after her previous strokes. Soon, Dad returned from his walk, passing the window and Mum gestured to him.

Next, she was smiling and waving to some children that we know. Children always made Mum smile, she loved them. Suddenly, Mum lost consciousness. We were distraught witnessing this. She didn't appear to respond to any stimuli. We telephoned for an ambulance right away. Mum was breathing and we checked her airway and looked for other signs like when she had strokes before.

It seemed an age before the ambulance arrived. Dad and I went along with Mum. The technicians were very busy, it was a stressful environment and there appeared to be monitors and apparatus everywhere. This seemed a different situation than before somehow. Dad and I watched helplessly, sitting in a shocked state of silence whilst they worked on her.

I prayed silently, hoping with all my heart that this would help. Seriously, how much more could she take, even if she did pull through again? Life is so tough and sometimes so unfair. My dad was visibly upset and I tried to keep strong and be of support.

When we arrived at the hospital, Mum was assessed in the emergency room. She had not regained consciousness yet. Would she? We were told to prepare ourselves. Was that white feather that fell in front of me earlier a sign from heaven? My brother came to the hospital straight away and my sister would be making her way shortly. She had a long journey ahead from Kent.

There were several doctors and nurses assessing and monitoring Mum. Finally, a Consultant took my dad, brother and I into a private room and advised that there would be no investigations, treatments or interventions this time. Mum would be placed on The Liverpool Care Pathway. She was now a dying patient.

Richard came back and to from the hospital with food, refreshments and other provisions. It was a huge comfort to know that he was taking great care of Daisy and also Charlie in between these trips. This poor dog was especially distressed having seen Mum departing from home in an ambulance and his caregiver (Dad) was leaving at a time of crisis, and in such an anxious state.

By the time my sister arrived at the hospital with little Jessica, my niece, Mum was settled in a private room. She looked as though she were sleeping. I remember seeing Jessica give "Ganny" a kiss goodnight. There were no tubes, noisy monitors or suchlike and Mum looked quite comfortable. I sincerely hoped that she was. Jessica wasn't at all upset or frightened in this environment.

We were told that Mum would not pass immediately and were advised to go home. The nurses said we needed rest, but how could we? There was no way that I was going to leave her here, alone. I was staying put.

My sister took Jessica back to my parents' home to get something to eat and settle her for the night. It had been a long journey for my brother-in-law Graham, Kate and little Jessica.

I had a strong disinclination to eat, however Richard was soon back with Kate in tow and yet more food and refreshments for us all. He insisted that we all took something to eat, just a little, which was yielding to the demands of exhaustion, and not of appetite. Dad was pale with worry and weariness. No doubt I was comparable. Richard had kindly brought along a small Lapis Lazuli crystal angel that I had requested. My friend Cheryl had given this to me when Dexter passed away. Richard didn't query or question when I asked for this.

We sat on the plastic hospital chairs until our bottoms were numb, not daring to leave mum's bedside. We eventually went individually, one by one for a little walk to stretch our legs, or to use the toilet facilities, Mum looked peaceful, resting. She was dressed in some of her own lovely clean and crisp, well ironed pyjamas. She looked beautiful and certainly didn't look her age. The stress and pain had now been lifted from her face.

Richard left us and returned to check on little Daisy and Charlie. Eventually, after some time, my brother and sister reluctantly said that they were going to go back home to get some rest. Although the nurses tried to persuade Dad and me to do the same, we would not leave. They advised us that Mum could go on for days like she was. Since the room next to Mum was vacant, a good-natured nurse offered this bed to my dad, who looked badly in need of a lie-down.

I remained with Mum in her room, seated in a high back chair next to the window. It was getting late and I was in need of some rest too. I played some gentle music on my phone to soften the silence. I use this when doing Angelic Reiki, which is a holistic therapy that I am trained to do. Mum liked listening to this music, especially as it had no words and was relaxing. In a flash, I had nodded off in the chair.

What must have been a short while later, I felt a nudge. A gentle nudge. It felt like Dexter, how he would gently press his nose against me. I jumped up abruptly, wondering where I was. Was I dreaming? I soon realised that I wasn't as I glanced around the hospital room and had strong inclination that Mum was about to die. This feeling was beyond words. Was Dexter Mum's leading light?

I went over to Mum and noticed that her breathing had changed slightly. Clutching my little angel, I dashed out into the corridor in an attempt to get the attention of a nurse, who was briskly walking along the corridor. The nurse hadn't seen me so I silently raced after her. I didn't want to shout and wake up any patients. When I caught up with the nurse, I calmly stated that I thought my mum was about to pass over. The nurse was clearly very busy and explained that she was absolutely sure this would not be the case, not yet. She had been in to check, just a short while ago.

I was persistent, hassling her to come quickly. She tried again to reassure me. I was insistent; this was such a strong feeling/intuition. The nurse must have thought I was silly, but to put my mind at rest, she abandoned her duties and came back with me to examine dear Mum. Dad was wide awake by now, after hearing our voices. The three of us walked the remainder of the distance to Mum's room together. Yes, the nurse could hear that Mum's breathing had now changed, especially since it had now also become amplified. We were advised to notify my brother and sister and not to worry.

Dad and I held Mum's hands. I was still holding my angel whilst sitting quietly beside her. The window was ajar and the blinds swished ever so slightly with in the cool night air entering the room. It was close to midnight and everywhere felt really still and quiet, despite being in this hospital environment. I said a silent prayer for a peaceful, pain free passing for Mum, respectfully requesting that she would be well looked after.

Quite literally a moment or two later, she slipped away and departed. It was that quick. We sat in silence not wanting to leave her, listening for breathing that wasn't there. Had Mum really gone? The nurse returned and confirmed that she had. Dad was noticeably grief stricken but we drew some comfort from the fact that Mum died so peacefully especially after all the pain that she endured over recent years. She had stoic courage and remarkable strength of character.

When Richard and my brother and sister arrived at the hospital, Mum's body was still warm, but her soul had departed. My siblings were heartbroken, devastated in fact to have left the hospital and not been there at the time of her passing. But this could not be changed now,

Mum was gone, and this must have been how it was to be. Emotions run high at such a time, but I kept my composure. I felt privileged to be with Mum and be of support to Dad. We had been through a lot recently. I asked my brother and sister if they wanted to hold the little crystal angel, as I believe that this held some of Mum's energy, her vibration, having been with her at her time of death. Stones absorb energy and I hope it comforted them. They had wanted to physically be with Mum, and I felt I had to offer something to console them. Perhaps they thought I had lost the plot. Regardless, this was done with good intention.

Richard and I eventually arrived back at the bungalow (camper) having spent time over at Dad's house immediately after returning from the hospital. It really hit home now that despite all our efforts, all the hard work and planning, Mum was never going to live here. This made me sad thinking about how much Mum and Dexter would have benefited from living in the bungalow but also made me think, how much fun they would be having together now. Now that they were free from any pain and restriction. They would have a ball and yes Dexter would probably be playing with one too.

Once again little Daisy, our cat, helped us all enormously in the days, weeks and months that followed. Although I endured their absence, Daisy helped me to avoid being overwhelmed with sadness, because I missed Dexter and Mum so very much. Richard and I had inadvertently taken our foot off the gas with regard to renovations, as seemingly there was no rush to move into the bungalow now. We had lots to sort out following Mum passing away. I was sluggish because of exhaustion and pain. It was not easy to get things done.

There was drama, emotional turbulence and upset with regard to the burial of Mum's ashes. This was firstly due to a stubborn and most intolerant and inconsiderate vicar not wanting to allow a plot. However, with a pleading letter to the church, respectfully requesting them to reconsider and fulfil their promise that had been made some years ago, all was sorted. I'm sure divine intervention played a part and hopefully Mum was eventually at peace.

The interment of ashes is the act of placing cremated remains in a final resting place, a permanent location. In mum's case this was the church cemetery. Family members only were present, that's what Dad wanted. However, the ceremony didn't quite go as planned. Unfortunately, the funeral arranger tripped, fell down onto her knees (in the mud). This happened when the reading was being conducted by the vicar who officiated. It was scarily like a comedy sketch. Mum's wooden ashes box dropped into the plot and landed at a precarious angle.

Blimey, it was, once again, one of those situations where everyone looks at each other, not knowing what to say or how to react. On the way out of the cemetery gates my sister commented awkwardly "Mum would have laughed", to which I replied "no, she would have tutted". We all laughed nervously then. Mum had got into a lot of trouble for 'tutting' when she was younger, but that's another story! She would seriously not have been impressed at being launched into a burial plot, but Mum also had a great sense of humour. I sincerely hope that she would have seen the funny side too.

With regards to the bungalow, Daisy the previously 'feral' hardy barn cat, had decided we were ready to move in. We had some deck chairs in the bungalow to sit on when we were having a break from renovations, decorating and such like. Daisy loved to sit on one of these chairs and actually slept on one overnight. You might recall that we had previously been told that this cat would never move into a house? Hmmm. Daisy encouraged us to start moving in.

Without further ado we installed a cat flap into the glass of one of the bi-fold doors. Richard made a step so that Daisy had easy access in and out, which she very much appreciated. Daisy loved our home and she filled our home with love. She came to and fro with her significant presence, carefully observing and monitoring activities.

Daisy loved climbing the timbers installed for the new stud walls, exploring kitchen cabinets and of course climbing ladders to get up and down from the loft space.

She continued to 'manage' all operations checking deliveries daily, even to the extent that she went up on a builder's merchant's crane on one occasion. Delivery drivers and tradesmen were fascinated watching her slide down the windscreens of their vehicles having climbed up onto the roof. With Daisy's help we were unquestionably back on track, and soon moved in. We went on walks around the paddock together, every day without fail. She even encouraged me to start writing.

I had more time on my hands after Mum passed away. When my physical health improved to a point where I felt able, I worked part-time locally and I walked to work to keep mobile. I also continued to help people and their animals with communications. I didn't advertise or use social media. Word spread far and wide. People requested help with their animals and were intrigued and enlightened hearing/seeing their pets' point of view. The effect and outcome can often be transformational to both the animal and owner which is truly wonderful to see. Many animal charities and those in need have benefited from my animal communications. It was, has and always will be a privilege to help with an open mind and an open heart.

I rather hope that speaking out about animal communication and bringing to the forefront through Dexter's story, this will help many more animals and people. Mum understood, she was behind me and desperately wanted me to write this book. I hope that Dexter's legacy will resonate with all reading Dexter's Diaries. The whole process has been reflective, purposeful and cathartic and has given me an enormous sense of accomplishment knowing Dexter will be forever immortalised in print.

15

TWO BY TWO

I had a dream one night where Dexter was leading me to a lady that is a Psychic/Medium. She is an extremely gifted lady with whom I had a reading some years previously. The dream didn't actually make sense to me, but I decided to contact Lesley and tell her who and what I had seen, and to explain about her 'teaching'. The dream was so vivid.

I looked up her number and plucked up the courage to pick up the telephone, only to put it down again. This was a highly respected Psychic/Medium. Would she even listen to me? Not truly understanding exactly why I was doing this, I picked up the phone and actually dialled her number this time, hoping that she could fathom this out. No doubt she would think it was crazy.

Lesley answered the call right away and she listened intently whilst I felt foolish bumbling on. She then explained to me that she did actually 'teach' many years ago but no longer did so now. She took this information (from me) as a nudge that she should start teaching again. Lesley said she would be in touch when she started up the 'circle'. I didn't understand …a circle? What was all this? That's when I 'heard' my inner voice telling me that it would be "more credible if you did humans too"?! Oh golly what had I done now?

I understand that people have psychic ability or a high sense of intuition at different degrees – whether we develop this or not will depend on us. The word psychic is derived from the Greek word 'psychikos' relating to the soul or mind. I guess all of us receive psychic impressions (telepathy) to some extent, such as knowing who is calling you on the telephone before you pick up and answer. You think about someone you haven't seen for ages and then see them.

Some people say that intuitive abilities are often genetically passed on, and that children are naturally intuitive and sensitive. I believe this is the case for a number of my nieces. Millie, in particular, has experienced feeling/perception of what is not normally perceptive. Perhaps this connection runs in our family. However, I must stress, regardless of whether people are believers or sceptics, living in the 'real world' Dexter certainly gave me a new perspective on life.

Lesley contacted me as she had promised. I discovered that natural psychics and mediums can benefit by developing their gifts in a disciplined mediumship circle. It is called a "circle" because people actually sit in a circle. The seating arrangements were determined by Lesley. I took my assigned seat on that first evening and decided to embrace this experience. I was a little nervous initially as one sometimes is in a new situation. I soon settled in knowing that the group, were, after all, embarking on a journey just like me. Regardless of experience (or not) I carried on, with nothing to lose.

Lesley guided the group with her extensive knowledge and experience. I found that I was comfortable expressing authenticity by communicating with both animals and people, but felt I was very much a novice in this arena. The exercises were varied and some were challenging, but I enjoyed it. Of course anyone can get things wrong or mishear. We are after all, only human.

In a safe environment, I feel that it is important to pass on what you hear (Clairaudience) which actually means 'clear hearing', (Clairvoyance) 'clear seeing' or feel (Clairsentience) 'clear physical feeling'. Even if what you receive appears somewhat foolish, as I mentioned previously, I believe that it is important to have the courage to divulge. We learn a great deal from our experiences and as with animal communication, invariably information will make sense to the person for whom the message is intended. People really do sit up and listen when something is revealed that only they could know.

Dexter was instrumental in my development and I

am sure that he was assisting and guiding me immensely all the way, through all of my experiences.

I learnt a lot from Lesley. Goodness knows what ever she thought of all the animals coming through to the circle as a result of me being there though. Lesley's beautiful Boxer dog was included in this menagerie. I was delighted to pass this information on to her and have it validated too. This was high praise indeed.

It always made me smile when Lesley found she had animals queuing up for me …she would say "Joanne …I have two ducks here for you". Then go on to describe them in exacting detail. "Joanne, a couple of cats for you tonight". So on and so on!

After some time, Lesley moved locations. She went back to live in the place where she grew up and still practises there now. As this was too far for me to travel each week, my time at the circle sadly was complete. However, some of the animals that she described did materialise. In ways I could never have imagined.

Life went on and I enjoyed the part-time, regular, employment that I started after Mum passed away but ended up leaving this office based work after a while. I found it wasn't good for me to sit for periods of time, even though I wasn't using a computer for lengthy portions of time. Sitting aggravated my condition and made my spine, nerve and joint problems deteriorate further.

To help keep active, I started doing a little dog

walking for people that I know and those who requested my help. That's where some of the dogs that Lesley predicted would be in my life, came into the equation. I love to be in the company of animals, especially dogs of course. I so missed walking with Dexter. So, this was beneficial all round.

Exercise and routine are good. Dogs love it too, but I have to be careful not to overdo things. Because of Dexter I learnt to listen to my body. In the past, I pushed myself past exhaustion. Now I take things slowly and do try to stop when my physical condition signals to do so. I do feel that it's important to keep mobile wherever possible, since I am not able to engage in the variety of activities that I used to. I try my best to take responsibility for my health but recognise some circumstances are beyond my control. It's important for me to best that I can be so that I can assist in looking after everyone here.

Richard and I have some additions/dependants to love and care for. After well over 20 years of marriage, we finally have 'kids', kid goats to be precise. Also ducks. Daisy has willingly accepted these additions into our family. They do not need to share her personal space, so she doesn't feel threatened in any way like she did whilst penned up in the rescue centre. It is so lovely to see our paddocks being used. I am sure that Dexter will approve.

This latest adventure came about after visiting a 'petting farm' with my nieces. Some goats were being bottle fed and whilst sitting there observing these beautiful creatures, I was prompted to ask what happens to the baby goats when they are grown up. I was taken to one side and told "they get slaughtered".

I was troubled by this and asked if they would kindly contact me should any of the farm animals need a home. I received a list by email of 'surplus stock'. There was a young male goat on the list. He was some sort of pygmy that needed a home because otherwise he was going to be slaughtered. He wasn't wanted because he was a boy and was an accident.

I spoke with Richard and got the signature 'look' again! He would need to make a stable, and secure fencing too so I was dubious. Nevertheless, he agreed this was the right thing to do. Of course we would have to have at least two goats; they are herd animals and need at least one of their kind so I had a chat with the farm manager who was friendly and accommodating about our situation. It would be so lovely to see the paddocks used. We already had hay stored in the barn which was taken off the field by a local farmer the previous year. There were a couple of ducks listed. One had been attacked by a bird of prey and had a hole in her head. Could we offer her and her companion a home, a safe place too?

Richard and I visited the farm to meet the animals and arrange a convenient date to collect. The farm staff looked bemused when I said we would most likely transport them home (approximately 40 minutes) in the back of our Jeep. We had assisted a lady who ran a goat rescue on a previous occasion and she used a Jeep herself to transport animals on many occasions. She said the goats felt safer in a smaller space like this.

I think a trailer would have been a preferable option from the farm staff point of view, but our Jeep was safe and probably would be more comfortable. I had an agreement with the farm manager that we would purchase another goat from the herd to keep the little male company. His mother had kindly been offered to us. However, the girl who was designated to show us around did not know which one she was. We were told there was a paddock full of females as we made our way through the yard. The girl did not know what she looked like, just that she was young and the kid was 'an accident'.

Silently, I asked for the mother of the little male goat to make herself known. I asked that should she be in agreement and want to come and live with us, to make it obvious who she was. Animals are quick to pick up our thoughts and words.

En route the young farm worker girl took a call on her mobile. Richard was not impressed by the operation here. I took the opportunity to tell him what I had suggested to the female goat. He was now keen to arrange possession of 'our' animals.

We walked through another barn which was a children's soft play area. Out through the back we walked, and into a large field split up into several paddocks. There were a variety of species. The first paddock contained a herd of pygmy type goats. All females. One was standing to the left hand side, well away from all the others who were climbing the wire in the hope of food. This was Monday when the farm was closed to the general public and I guessed that they thought it might well be their lucky day?

I looked at the lone female and quite literally my heart melted. Tears came to my eyes and I said to the girl "that's her". She said she did not know but would go and check and toddled off once more. This little goat was so beautiful and so full of love.

Being able to communicate with animals helps me to pick up on and understand emotions as well as physical issues (or both). It goes without saying only a vet can diagnose. Animal communication should never ever be a substitute for veterinary examination, diagnosis and treatment. Dexter helped me immeasurably and I learned so much because of his insights and love. He was the greatest teacher undoubtedly I will ever have.

Richard looked at me and he knew too that this little girl was the one for us. She had such a sweet, gentle energy and as it happens, yes she was the young mother of the little lad. This brings me to Sonny. Next we were taken to a paddock with highland cattle, sheep and a bad tempered fully grown Billy goat who was not at all happy sharing his space with a growing kid.

What a sorry sight. It was starting to rain and this paddock was already beyond boggy under foot. The little goat was not permitted to enter the tiny plastic shelter which was in no way adequate to house and protect all of these animals from the elements. Richard and I went to the fence to take a closer look. The little bedraggled boy came over but was butted up in the air by the bad tempered Billy. The kid landed with an almighty bang on his side, hitting his head in the process. He looked very sad, listless and depressed. I felt so much sadness and despair. Richard looked disgusted, seeing the animals living like this.

We looked at the ducks next, there were four amongst the chickens but two were 'surplus stock'. There was no water to bathe in, just a bowl and chicken drinker to drink from. One little duck just went around in circles. She had been attacked by a bird of prey and had an injury to her head. The farm staff had thrown a chick in to the paddock as bait in an attempt to save this duck. Fortunately, for her it worked. The two ducks were gorgeous. A bonded pair, pure white Campbell's. I blurted out "let's call them Dolly and Daydream". We could see that they were clearly devoted to each other. They also looked exactly like the ducks that Lesley had described. Richard and I agreed a date with the farm manager to come back and collect our flock.

Back at home, all hands were on deck to prepare. Richard designed and built suitably appropriate housing and my dad helped with some of the work. It helped to take dad's mind off things as his dog had sadly recently passed away. A lot of thought went into this preparation work, rightly so, as every animal, whether that be farm or domestic, deserves to be treated with kindness and have a home that provides for all their needs to be met.

Whilst building was underway I sought veterinary advice regarding Sonny, soon to be our 'kid' goat. He would need to be castrated if he was going to share a paddock with his sweet and gentle mother. Hormones are a huge issue. This procedure needed to be done right away before the goats were moved, for obvious reasons!

I also asked the vet whether she could kindly take a good look at Sonny when she visited the farm. I mentioned that I did not feel that he was in good health and asked when giving him the once over could she please check his stomach, in particular. I explained I was not knowledgeable at all about goats but just had a 'feeling'. To appease me, she said she would take a 'muck' sample when she carried out the castration procedure at the farm.

Sonny was then duly castrated. I received a telephone call to confirm that all was well in this department. A muck sample had also been taken and the results were in. The vet had never seen such a high result. Coccidia was, in her words 'off the scale'. He was full of parasites.

Sonny needed urgent medication to treat the symptoms of coccidiossis and he needed it now. She shocked me by saying that he needed this medication in the next 48 hours or else he would die.

Because of the call out charges involved, our vet suggested we pick up the medications, contact the farm, and request that the herdsmen administer the injections, or alternatively, carry this out ourselves. I asked the farm manager for assistance with this, but was disappointed to hear that they were too busy. Furthermore, they would not allow Richard or I to administer them which is what our vet had suggested.

I called the vet and asked her to please go out again. She was totally and utterly dismayed, but what else could we do. One would have thought that animal welfare would come first on a farm. Evidently, children's parties and getting everywhere ready for all the half term events was priority at this time.

It was a bit of a race against time to get everything ready. Finally the day arrived, a new beginning for our gang. My father-in-law, Rob, was staying with us for a few days and he wanted to come along with us today. He proudly donned his flat cap for the occasion. Rob's father had a smallholding and he had fond memories recounting stories of looking after geese and hens when he was a child.

Richard and I filled the heavy duty plastic boot liner in the Jeep full of straw. I selected the most appropriately sized animal carrier we owned to transport the ducks, and positioned it onto the back seat. Daisy waited patiently. The roles of the animals had been determined already. Goats for entertainment, ducks providers of food (eggs), and Daisy was of course, Management.

Controversially the farm staff could not believe we really did not bring a trailer along to transport the animals. They must have thought that we joking about the Jeep. After we had paid the agreed fee, they were open mouthed watching us drive away. Everyone, to their surprise, had loaded fine and were calm and settled. I sat next to the girls (ducks in the carrier) and kept a check on the goats by turning my head and looking through Dexter's rear dog guard.

I suggested that we should call our girl goat Twinkle. She had what looked like a little star on her forehead. I used to read 'Twinkle' comic when I was a young girl and this name instantly suited her. Of course I had checked with her it was ok. Sonny snuggled up against his mum, Twinkle. It was so nice to see them reunited, albeit in the back of a car. It felt surreal driving along.

I was beaming looking around. Two goats (with horns) in the boot and the ducks right next to me. I started to chuckle. Then began to sing an adapted version of 'Kids' the Kylie Minogue and Robbie William's song..

"Ducks on board, take a ride (yeah)

Ducks on board, feel the high (yeah)

'Cause the kids are alright!"

Richard and his dad were in hysterics.

Our little flock was brilliantly behaved on the journey home, no windows or upholstery damaged by horns. No crying, nervousness, quacking or flapping. When we arrived safely at home, Daisy was waiting. She had selected the very best place to observe and manage our herd. We used Dexter's ramp for the goats to safely trot down, out of the car boot, and into the paddock. It worked a treat. The goats enjoyed tucking into the hay that we had made readily available for their arrival. In their own time, the ducks waddled out of their carrier and enjoyed bathing in the bath that Richard had purposely built for them. They all settled beautifully in the paddock they were sharing together.

The vet came to visit a few days later with supplementary medication. The goats also need antibiotics for infections and treatment for mites. The poor souls were riddled with mites. Sonny was practically hairless. He had no undercoat because he had rubbed himself so much. With the benefit of the pain killer also administered, they were soothed and comfortable.

Living harmoniously together, they are now almost unrecognisable from their condition when they arrived. Although Sonny does have his moments. The vet advised that genetics and trauma resulting from being beaten and butted by the bully Billy would not have helped. Sonny has neurological/inflammation issues too but despite this, he is thriving. The vet had said when she first came out to visit, that Sonny would always be little, weedy and thin. This is categorically not the case. He is almost on the plump side now. This is pleasing, since the vet advised that Pygmy types should actually look like this. Sonny towers over his beautiful mother and he is still young. They are both gorgeous creatures.

The goats thick, full coats shine now on account of a nutritious organic goat feed, supplemented with herbs and vitamins. They enjoy delicious fresh produce too, including fresh fruit and vegetables. They have in excess of their 'five a day' and if I'm totally honest, eat better than we do. In the supermarket recently a lady saw me loading bananas that were on special offer into my trolley. She commented, "Do you have monkeys?" I smiled, and replied "Yes, that's one word to describe them". A little love and a banana certainly do go a long way.

At the time of writing this, Richard is actually in the process of building bigger housing. Who will be coming next, I wonder? We have been avid supporters of the Donkey Sanctuary for many years and have been 'home-checked'. So, fingers, paws, hooves and wings crossed that someday, if/when the time is right, and all the works are complete, and circumstances permit, we may possibly have another species to join our family.

We have learned a great deal about animal husbandry on this journey. The knowledge that Dexter imparted has been instrumental to the health and well being of our animal family. We still consult his diary for reference. Dexter would have loved living here with our ducks. He was fascinated by feathered friends and these are super little characters. Loving mealworms, kale, lettuce and a little cider vinegar soaked bread. They bomb over, gobble up and thoroughly deserve these treats from us, they are such little superstars.

Would you believe that they once saved the village of damaging effects from fire? Having alerted me, in the first instance, to raise the alarm, well before anything was visible, the raging fire was quickly contained, which unquestioningly helped to stop the spread. Despite there being no acknowledgement for the ducks in the fire report, this was remarkable. I must stress, that animals in general, have such an amazing intuitive ability to sense and act on frequencies around them. For example, you may notice your pets acting strangely if there is a thunderstorm on the way. They sense danger and can also feel if something is wrong with you too. Our ducks sensed danger of fire. Not so long after this incident, which was incidentally, very close to our home, we sadly lost one of our ducks, Dolly.

One Saturday morning, I was in the paddock tending to everyone and got a totally overwhelming feeling that Dolly was going to die. It made me stop in my tracks. I called Richard over to the fence; he was over by the bungalow. I told him what I felt. He looked at me like I was mad. It was in fact true that Dolly had been running around with Daydream just a few minutes earlier. I urged Richard to come into the paddock, "I'm serious" I shouted. So, in sensing my tone he dutifully complied. He knelt down when he reached us, and did not question me further. He picked dear Dolly up.

I stroked Dolly as he held her. Suddenly, just like that she passed away in Richard's arms. She was gone, peacefully and naturally. We were mortified, but I guess comforted in a way. She was active to the last, did not suffer, and had a dignified end. Dolly knew that she was dearly loved and I really hope that helped her.

We cradled her beautiful body for a short while, and then placed her in an open box in the paddock so that her companions could see her. If possible, I feel it is helpful for surviving animals to be given the opportunity to view a body, to say goodbye if they want to, just like we do in a chapel of rest with a loved one. Sometimes sniffing and examining the body helps animals to understand, and to come to terms with what has happened. They can then grieve in their own way.

Dolly had led the way always. She was such a support to Daydream. Thankfully, Daydream's head had healed and she no longer went around in circles but she relied on Dolly. The girls were always busy and running around the paddock. To now see this poor girl, standing totally motionless, staring at Dolly's lifeless body was heartbreaking.

The goats respectfully observed Dolly, and Daisy did

too. We eventually removed the box from the paddock and covered her with hay and some flowers before closing. Richard was visibly upset. He utterly adores our ducks. Working for the fire service, Richard is subjected to a lot of trauma, but this still affected him greatly. As much as I believe that animals come into our lives to teach us to love, and to teach us about loss, I could not think about this now. I had to get a grip and act fast. No way could we leave Daydream to cope on her own while she grieved, or she would die of a broken heart, if we did not get her some help today. I could feel this. She simply was not a personality to cope without a companion. Saving Daydream was now a priority.

I set about ringing animal rescue centres. I was upset that no-one would even consider letting two paired ducks go, out of the established flocks that they had. We could not take more than two ducks today because our duck housing could only comfortably accommodate four in the sleeping quarters.

Our girls had housing, purpose built to ensure a comfortable environment, with plenty of space to move, eat and drink throughout the night. We could not have any overcrowding. Besides, Daydream being such a laid back, gentle character might not cope with an already established group. I tried further afield, and disappointingly, from every centre came the same response. I wonder could this be the reason that some places are overrun.

I was going to have to purchase a duck from a breeder to provide company for Daydream. Hopefully a youngster, so that Daydream would not be bullied herself. Trawling the internet, I found a breeder almost an hour away. However, when I called the gentleman, I discovered he was travelling back from his holiday destination. He was four hours away in West Wales. I explained our predicament and he compassionately and willing gave his time and advice freely. He agreed that Daydream needed company immediately. At last sense from a caring and honest breeder. John (the duck breeder) would not reach home until after seven pm. We could go then.

It was only when I put the phone down, that I remembered that my friend Fiona, who I actually met on Amelia Kinkade's animal communication course, was coming to stay with us tonight and would be arriving around six-thirty. Fiona was on her way from Somerset, but I was sure she would not mind coming along with us. I telephoned and checked of course. Despite her long journey, she was more than happy to go with us. Fiona understood. She is lovely, an accomplished chiropractor who works with animals. She has her own farm and beautiful animals too.

So Fiona arrived, we all bolted down something to eat and off we trekked. Richard, Fiona and I, complete with cat carrier to collect a companion to comfort Daydream. This was absolutely the right thing to do.

Poor Daydream was still rooted to the spot where she settled this morning. She is normally very active.

Fiona and I enjoyed catching up and chatting on the journey. It was a race against time, as we had to be back and home before dark. Ducks are vulnerable to attack from predators such as foxes. Almost all of our neighbours' chickens came to an untimely end after they were attacked by a mink. Although Daisy has been known to chase off predators, and we have the goats to assist too, we would never risk leaving our beloved ducks out after sundown.

When we arrived at the breeder's smallholding, John was waiting as promised. What a lovely chap. He took us to see his ducks. He asked us, from the flock of approximately thirty young ducks, would we kindly like to select one and he would then check the sex. Both Richard and I pointed to the same duck. John and Fiona were flabbergasted but there was no time for explanations. John checked and yes of course, she was the one and a girl too. A gorgeous one at that. All white feathers like Daydream, but with a very bright yellow beak. She was a 'Cherry Valley' duck. A hybrid cross breed of Peking and Aylesbury. A Jemima Puddle Duck.

Under different circumstances, we could have chatted to John all night. He was so knowledgeable, amicable and had a stunt boat used in a James Bond film! Richard was very impressed. We left swiftly, along with some grower's food for Dilys as she was still young. Putting

Dilys in the car was a bitter-sweet moment. This lovely girl travelled quietly and calmly in the cat carrier next to me.

When we arrived home Richard carefully took the carrier, from the car to the paddock. It was just starting to go dark. Daydream was still solemnly sitting in the exact same spot until ... Dilys emerged from the carrier. As if by magic, Daydream sprung to life and the two ducks greeted each other with an excitable quack. They proceeded to bomb around the entire paddock together. Daydream longed for a friend, and these two quickly got along and would not leave each other's side. What a relief it was beautiful to see. Twinkle and Sonny also took to Dilys like a duck to water.

All of us will always be indebted to Dexter. We are all living here because of Dexter, and we celebrate the meaning and purpose that he gave having opened up my life to a new way of thinking and living. I adore all the animals and I love to spend time with them. It gives me a lot of enjoyment. We are delighted that all our fur and feathered family are bonded and have found friendship with each other under Daisy's management. Every day, without fail we enjoy 'family walks', headed up by Daisy on the outside perimeter of the paddock.

Richard sometimes gets the mickey taken out of him by local people and neighbours (especially if he goes to the pub). It's light-hearted and good-natured humour for those who have seen us with our animals. I guess it's not an everyday sight or occurrence that people have pet ducks, goats and a previously feral cat that heads up walks. Regardless, we value our little family, they are characters in their own right. They love human-interaction and I feel that it's an honour that they all actually want to be close to us.

Many studies have been conducted on how human-animal interaction influences both our physical and mental health. Animals can have a positive impact on our lives and help us all in so many ways. I would just like to mention my dad's dog in this respect. Dad is super resilient and fiercely independent and after almost fifty years of marriage he understandably struggles on to adapt to life without Mum. Dad suffered two strokes himself, after losing her and then his beloved dog Charlie passed away. Jay (his special little dog) now keeps him going and has a huge impact on his health and wellbeing.

Jay is a petite black Labrador, a beautiful ex-breeder with a super temperament; she is so attentive to Dad. I just knew that they would connect and help each other. I felt compelled to engineer their introduction and I am so glad that I did. Jay loves her new home, a nutritious diet, regular walks and socialisation. Jay evidently appreciates this blissful and peaceful retirement environment away from the breeding kennels.

She copes with absolutely every situation; she is a joy to be around and is a treasured companion for Dad. All our family adores Jay, in fact anyone who meets her does. Considering her past, after previously living with seventeen other kennelled dogs, her ability to love people is amazing. Jay makes home a happy and loving environment for Dad. She is a wonderful addition to the family and has truly helped him more than any human possibly ever could. Dad lives for Jay and sweet, little Jay is devoted to Dad. She has brought much pleasure and greatly enriched his life. I am absolutely certain of that.

Jay and our little Daisy cat, are both shining examples of companion animals that didn't start off sharing their lives closely with humans. I am so thankful to these two super girls, and of course all of the animals that I have had the privilege of getting to know and the pleasure of communicating with.

Every single one is special. Every single one loved. I really appreciate their belief in me and I am particularly grateful to them for putting their trust in me. Ultimately, all is attributed to Dexter. He has had an immense impact on all our lives.

It is my wish that this book will go a little way to help you and your animal friends, along the path that all of us are, at some point or other (whether human or animal), likely to tread. Seriously, I completely understand that no book can ever make up for the heartache of bereavement. However, I believe that Dexter's beautiful soul lives on and writing *Dexter's Diary*, has helped me to carry on his wishes. I hope that this book will inspire others when struggling with illness, grief or loss. Whatever species they may be.

I appreciate that tears will come, even after decades have passed. But so too will laughter. Reliving the special and ordinary times that we spend is precious. These memories bring comfort and will never be forgotten. In our case, especially so, as these are now in print, before my very eyes. Before Dexter, I would never really have believed that I was capable of writing a book. He knew me better than I knew myself. He knew I could do it; he believed in me and predetermined my destiny. To have *Dexter's Diary* published is a dream come true.

I really do hope that you've enjoyed reading all about the dog that transformed my life. Dexter truly is my angel. He's the thread in the tapestry of my life. We have an abiding, unequivocal connection that knows no end. With gratitude and everlasting love, I believe whole-heartedly and passionately, that Dexter will always be with me, and forever in my heart.

I'm sure that this will be the case with you, and your loved ones too. This bond, the power of love that we share with our pets, really is so strong, that it can never be broken. Ever.

....This is not the end of our story.

Contact dexter@jjangels.co.uk to hear more about future publications by signing up for our email list.

www.jjangels.co.uk

LINKS

British Dalmatian Welfare www.dalmatianwelfare.co.uk
Bioflow Direct www.bioflow.com
Equafleece www.equafleece.co.uk
Hilton Herbs www.hiltonherbs.com
Orvis www.orvis.co.uk
Fish4dogs www.fish4dogs.com
Lesley Shepherd www.lesleyshepherd-medium.com
Jackie Weaver www.animalpsychic.co.uk
Amelia Kinkade www.ameliakinkade.com and
www.languageofmiraclesinstitute.com
Dr Fiona Pim, Connected Naturally www.
animalchiropractic.co.uk
www.manytearsrescue.org
dogfuriendly.com

Printed in Poland
by Amazon Fulfillment
Poland Sp. z o.o., Wrocław

59888472R00132